LOVE CHILD

LOVE CHILD
MY SURROGATE BABY

RONA WALKER

BLOOMSBURY

First published in Great Britain 1990
Bloomsbury Publishing Limited, 2 Soho Square, London w1v 5de

Copyright © 1990 by Linda Cameron

All photographs from the author's collection except
page 8: John Whitfield

A CIP catalogue record for this book
is available from the British Library

isbn 0–7475–0685–x

10 9 8 7 6 5 4 3 2 1

Typeset by Hewer Text Composition Services, Edinburgh
Printed and bound in Great Britain by
Butler and Tanner Ltd, Frome and London

To Kathleen and Emma.
Daddy and I love you both dearly.

ACKNOWLEDGEMENTS

Owing to the very nature of my story, few people knew the facts. But of those who did, first and foremost I must thank Stephanie. How can I find words to thank you? Have a wonderful life, you deserve it.

My heartfelt thanks go to Mrs Gena Dodd, who was always there with an answer when I needed her. I'd also like to say a special thanks to Professor Churchill and Susan (whose names have been changed in this book at their request) and to all the medical staff involved with my care at Aberdeen Royal Infirmary. Reverend Alan Swinton, the hospital chaplain, who was a guiding light in my darkest days, deserves a special mention.

My sincere thanks go to Lucy Smith, for her tireless patience, endurance and understanding in the writing of this book.

My deepest appreciation goes to Malcolm Brinkworth and Geoffrey Hamilton-Fairley, for all their professional advice and emotional support. In particular I am grateful to Malcolm, who for the past eighteen months has bullied and nagged me – and I still love him!

Last but not least, there are three very important people to thank: my dear mother and sister, who lived through it all with me, and my beloved husband, who picked up the pieces of my shattered life and so tenderly restored it.

CONTENTS

1
PREGNANT BEGINNINGS

The baby on the scan in front of me was full of life and busy with its own small, secret energy. I was amazed to see my womb was such a hive of activity and, as I watched, the words 'alive and kicking' suddenly took on new-minted meaning: the baby's legs were threshing, its arms were flailing, it waved and stretched its limbs in a silent, marvellous dance of life.

Thrilled, I watched as a small arm swung repeatedly up and down, reminding me irresistibly of the badminton games Mark and I had recently played.

'That's its badminton arm,' I said to the nurse, and we laughed.

Finding out now that I was definitely pregnant, seeing the baby there in my womb, I was out of this world with excitement and could have kissed the nurse. This would be my first baby: I'd never before experienced the sheer wonder of knowing that I could give life, or of seeing my child growing within me, a little marvel. A part of me, and a part of Mark, had fused forever, and this, this fragile fervent being, had flowered into life. I felt as if someone had lit a candle in my heart, so that my whole body glowed with love – for the baby; for Mark, who'd created it with me; and for life itself, from which could spring such unexpected, intensely joyful surprises.

The nurse passed the scanner slowly and carefully over my tummy, revealing every millimetre of the wee form inside. Checking the measurements, she estimated the baby was about twelve weeks old, suggesting a due date of around 17 October – my sister's birthday! She focused on each part of the baby in turn, and my wonder deepened with every detail. She pointed to the minute feet; the slender legs ceaselessly stirring; the waving arms with their furling fingers. Then she traced the small, sweet curve of the spine; the minuscule glory of the head; the soft swell of the chest. And there, diminutive, translucent, perfect, was the beating miracle of the heart with its pure, undeniable pulse.

I lay spellbound, scarcely able to move for delight. How long I watched, lost in amazement, I don't know; time was suspended, the ticking minutes had never seemed so irrelevant. Nothing mattered but this. As I saw the tiny child leaping and breathing inside me I felt such a surge of happiness it was as if not only the baby's, but my life, too, were just beginning.

Until that moment, I don't think I'd been conscious of just how deeply I wanted a child. True, I'd known for many years that eventually I'd like to settle down and have a family, but after an early marriage to my very first boyfriend came to grief after three years, I'd concentrated more on my career. My posts had taken me abroad as well as closer to home, and had been challenging enough so that I didn't have much time to dwell on whether I was truly fulfilled or not, or where my life was going. Yet as my middle twenties gave way to something nearer thirty, and then to thirty itself, I couldn't help noticing that most of my friends were already married and had children – not just babies, either, but fully-fledged schoolchildren, and several of them. Somewhere at the back of my mind I began to acknowledge that for all my hard and (occasionally) dynamic work, if I were honest with myself, I really felt that I was simply marking time until I too could marry and have a baby.

But at the time I really only let myself think this way now and then. Certainly, I hadn't got to the stage where I was in a blind panic and desperate to become pregnant at whatever cost. It wasn't as if I had to have a child to justify my existence: I was busy at work, and enjoyed an active social life. Until recently I'd been involved in a long-term relationship with a man for whom I cared dearly, and who cared for me. But somehow there had never been any question of us having children together. Much as I'd felt for Robert, deep down I'd known he wasn't the right person for me; there had always been a constraint between us which had stopped me from feeling completely at ease, and we had totally different values. At the time I couldn't explain clearly why, but eventually our relationship just died. I didn't know exactly what was lacking, nor precisely what I was looking for. All I knew was that this wasn't it.

In the months that followed I'd experienced both the regret and the relief that can come after the end of a long relationship. Regret, because we'd been together, on and off, for nearly four years, and there were many good things to remember; and relief because, single again, I felt a fresh zest for life. Though at thirty, I felt I could hardly pass myself off as a spring chicken, I was suddenly optimistic enough to feel that, no matter what had happened in the past, some day the right person would come along. I just began to wish he'd hurry up about it.

It was at this point, in July 1987, that I met Mark. He was a helicopter pilot for a well-established company, flying to and from the offshore oil rigs; I was working as office manager for an oil-related service company, so it was ironic that it wasn't work that brought us together. Instead, chance, and especially my sister, Megan, launched our relationship, though I must admit I played my part, too.

It all started one summer evening. I'd been on my own now for about five months, and was enjoying a night out with Megan at her favourite watering-hole, 'Ici'. She was obviously concerned at my lack of male company, and kept helpfully but unsuccessfully trying to draw various innocent men to my attention.

Her efforts seemed doomed to failure, when I suddenly spotted 'him' coming in. Very tall, very blond, and sporting a jacket that looked straight out of *Indiana Jones*, he was hardly easy to miss. Honesty doesn't permit me to claim it was love at first sight, but he was definitely a big improvement on Megan's potential candidates, and I promptly turned to my matchmaking expert and said jokingly, 'Well, on a scale of nought to ten, *he's* an eleven. So do something!'

Before I knew it, she was off. The place was packed, but from my vantage point I was just able to spy our

3

unsuspecting prey wandering upstairs, with Megan in hot pursuit pushing through the throng like a thing possessed. The press of people was too great, however, and I looked on helplessly as, blissfully unaware of the commotion and alcohol spillage he was causing, the object of our attentions drew further and further away from her and proceeded to stroll back downstairs and straight out the door.

Moments later, Megan reappeared. 'Damn!' she said. 'Lost him!'

I pointed to where he could just be glimpsed vanishing through the exit. She made one last valiant foray into the jungle of drinkers and dancers before returning defeated. We looked at each other, sighed, shrugged, and laughed. And that was the end of it. Or so I thought.

But, lo and behold, the very next day, a Sunday, Megan and I were down at the beach, setting off for a walk along the shore, when who should I spy but 'Him', strolling in our direction. I said to Megan, 'Isn't that that chap we saw last night?' and as we drew nearer, started leaping up and down, shrieking in a piercing whisper, 'It's him! It's him! Do something! Don't let him get away this time!' I should have realized then that something funny was happening to me, because I don't normally behave like this at all – I'm usually much more restrained, especially with people who are total strangers. Even on this occasion, nothing would have happened if it hadn't been for Megan. Looking back, it amazes me to think that, without her help, Mark and I would simply have walked straight past each other along that beach – and out of each other's lives.

But Megan had other ideas. Taking me at my word, she started to plot her strategy. We watched Mark go up to the pier to get an ice cream. Our plan – hardly a fiendishly sinister one – was to get behind him in the queue at the kiosk, and improvise from there. So we stood in the queue, and nothing happened. Megan didn't do anything, and I jabbed her in the ribs and muttered '*Do* something!'

Mark walked off and put his shoes in the car, and we followed him back down to the beach with as much discretion as we could muster, which wasn't a lot. As he was now barefoot, we knew he'd have to come back to the car eventually, so we decided to save our energy and lie in wait for him on his return, meanwhile topping up our tans and consuming our ice lollies. Though she gave no appearance of it, Megan must still have been plotting ways and means, for just as Mark hove into view once more she stood up on one of the wooden groins that juts into the sea and called in a very loud voice, 'D'you dare me to jump in fully clothed?'

Mark's highly romantic response was to ignore us totally and carry on walking. Without more ado, my brave sister promptly flung herself into the briny waves. I must mention here that even in high summer, the sea in our part of the world scarcely gives one what could be described as a warm welcome. On top of this, Megan's idea of 'fully clothed' in fact consisted of little more than a pair of shorts and a T-shirt. How she managed to escape instant hypothermia I'll never know. But escape it she did, which was fortunate because Mark was still resolutely uninterested: his receding back said it all. Waist-deep in the water and blueing around the lips, Megan abandoned any pretence of subtlety. 'Well,' she cried after him, 'did you enjoy yourself at Ici last night?'

Success! He stopped dead in his tracks, looked back, and came over to join us – Megan by this time having waded out of the sea, was standing on the sand trying to look cool (not too difficult, as she was freezing) and casual (rather more difficult) while salt water dripped off her hair and the end of her nose. The things a true sister will do for you . . . The three of us got chatting, and somehow managed to arrange to meet again at Ici that evening. And so it was that he was unwittingly ensnared.

Love is a strange thing. When I look back on that meeting, I can see that already, I must have felt more for Mark than I knew; at any rate, something was sparking me to behave like a teenager again. Or rather, like teenagers are supposed to behave, for I swear that even in my teens, *I'd* never done anything so forward and impulsive before. That impulsiveness and spontaneity were for me a very important element in our relationship. I'd never experienced anything like it. As the weeks went by, and Mark and I started to see each other nearly every day, my life was transformed. Parts of myself that I'd forgotten existed came bubbling up unexpectedly, more and more often. I'd find myself singing my little heart out as I drove home from seeing him. He was unlike anyone I'd ever met – so vital, so easy-going, such fun. For a start, the usual formalities attached to getting to know someone just didn't seem to exist for him: from the beginning, he'd walk straight into the flat in the morning, bacon and eggs in hand, and start cooking breakfast. He also – wonder of wonders – thought my jokes were funny. And if either of us had a whim, we could act on it: we took ballroom dancing classes in the evening and then went out and practised our steps together on the beach in the dark, much to the astonishment of late-night dog-walkers, their dogs, and the policemen out on the beat. Above all, we talked, and talked, and talked. Though I was some years older than him (I didn't tell him how many!), the affinity between us shrank that gap to nothing. Within a month, I knew I had found the person I'd been looking for all my life, though, having always been a cautious person, it took me a while to accept that all this was really happening. Coming from a previous relationship which was much more formal and supposedly 'sensible', I kept on expecting that there would be some hidden catch. But there was none.

And now, six months later, I was pregnant with our child. I felt truly complete, all of a sudden: it was joy, not the crisp February air, that made me catch my breath as I left the hospital after the scan. My only disappointment was that Mark hadn't been with me to see the baby. In fact he didn't even know I'd been sent for the scan. For this pregnancy was unplanned. Though our romance was something of a whirlwind one, I'd not abandoned my native caution entirely, and we'd been very careful; but accidents will happen . . .

The first inkling we'd had that something was up was when, a few weeks previously, I'd suffered a very heavy bleed, far heavier than my usual periods. I'd told Mark, and had consulted my doctor about it; but, although I'd been feeling slightly off-colour, he initially came to the conclusion that

I couldn't be pregnant, because of the bleeding. However, when I continued to feel slightly queasy, dizzy and tired, even though the bleeding had stopped, and my breasts had started to feel sore, I'd felt privately pretty convinced I was pregnant after all. I knew my own body, and couldn't accept his verdict. Eventually, I'd done a home pregnancy test. Sure enough, it came up positive: my instincts were right. Of course, I'd desperately wanted to tell Mark there and then, but the day I'd done the test was just before he was due to drive six hundred miles south to pick up some furniture from his parents, so I'd kept quiet because, though I was pretty sure he'd be pleased, I was worried the news might distract him so much from his driving, he'd have an accident!

Because he was travelling such a distance, he was staying with his parents for a few days to make the most of his trip. During this time I'd rushed back to my doctor, who'd performed another pregnancy test which also gave a positive result. Somewhat perplexed, the doctor had advised me that this might be because I'd suffered a miscarriage – which would account for the bleeding – and therefore my hormone level could still be high, producing a falsely 'positive' result. In order to make absolutely sure, he'd sent me for the scan.

In the day or so before I'd gone to the hospital, I'd been seized by a tumult of fear and confusion about what was happening inside my body. When I'd looked at that screen, I'd been half-afraid of what I might see: though I longed to see a baby there, I feared that instead there might be either nothing at all, or worse, something wrong. To see the baby was therefore a wonderful surprise, and it was especially precious to me, because the scan showed that I'd originally been expecting twins! While I'd been right to believe I was pregnant, my doctor had been correct in diagnosing a miscarriage: the scan showed some scar tissue where another baby had been lost about a fortnight before – around the time I had bled so heavily. Though I was sad to think of the lost twin, I was also full of joy to know the live baby was not only there, but thriving.

I couldn't wait to tell Mark. The only problem was, he'd still be away for another couple of days, so I was left on tenterhooks, bursting with this incredible news that I just wanted to shout from the rooftops. Although I didn't want anyone to know until I'd told him, I was so excited that I couldn't keep the news to myself for such a long time. Eventually I confided in my best friend, Angela, who was herself four or five months pregnant at the time. She was over the moon, and immediately got out the champagne; and we sat looking at it, not drinking a drop because we were both pregnant.

Somehow I managed to get through the next few days without telling anyone else, and without giving the game away to Mark each evening when we spoke on the phone. I so badly wanted him to be home safely I felt I just couldn't breathe a word of the news about the scan, because of him having to drive all those miles in the van. By the time he got back I was having palpitations with excitement – and with trepidation. For although I felt sure in my heart that he would feel as I did, I couldn't take it for granted; I had to have it clear, affirmed, in my head, and in this sense I was slightly tentative as to how he'd react. We'd only known each other for a short time, and, however wonderful those months had been, we hadn't yet begun to make long-term plans. Our relationship was so good, so natural and easy, that I didn't want to compromise Mark in any way.

In the end, I plucked up my courage that evening, and said, 'You know we suspected I might have had a miscarriage?'

'Yes.'

'Well, while you were away, I went for a scan, and unfortunately that was the case, I *did* miscarry . . .' Pause. He looked crestfallen. 'But there's another baby there! There were two, and this one's fighting fit!'

I remember Mark's face so clearly at that moment: his eyes lit up, he was like a little boy at Christmas. That one look sent any doubts I might have had about how he'd feel flying out the window. And he immediately said, 'We'll have to get married, as soon as possible.'

Though I couldn't have hoped for a response more in keeping with what I wanted most in the world, I had to be sure he wasn't doing this out of duty, so I said, 'No, no, we don't *have* to get married, we need to make sure this is what we both want . . .'

But it *was* what we both wanted; that much was obvious the more we talked about it, so we decided we would get married as soon as possible. And at one point that evening I said, 'Oh, is this my proposal then?'

Typically, Mark laughed and retorted, 'No, no. You'll have to wait a bit longer for that.'

A couple of weeks later we were lying in bed one night when Mark mentioned that he was a bit thirsty, and asked me to fetch him a drink from the fridge. I trotted off and opened it only to find an enormous bottle of Moët & Chandon with a great ribbon round it, and the bottle covered in lipstick saying, 'RONA RONA I LOVE YOU. PLEASE PLEASE MARRY ME!'

So I literally took my proposal back into bed with me.

For the next few weeks we were plunged into activity. We'd set the wedding day for the middle of May, and it was already early March, so there was a lot to get ready in a short space of time. As well as the hurly-burly of the wedding preparations, we still had a great deal of work to do on our flat; now that we knew I was pregnant, we had to do many things that, in the normal run of events, we'd have put off until later.

On top of all this, we both had jobs to hold down. I planned to carry on working until August before taking maternity leave. Until recently, this decision wouldn't have posed any problems, but for the past few months things at work had been deteriorating, and I wasn't relishing the prospect of struggling through five more months of feeling miserable while at the same time getting more and more heavily pregnant. On the other hand, with only this relatively short stint to work out before I could leave, it seemed silly to stop there and then, especially as financially we could do with the extra salary as we were in for an expensive year.

Now I wish with all my heart that I had left then, and spared myself a lot of grief. For those weeks between March and May were a hellish time. Originally I'd been very happy in my job, but since about Christmas of 1987 all that had changed. Basically, the problem was my boss. From being a delightful, easy-going man to work for, with a totally open-door style of management, he'd turned into what I can only describe as a tyrant. We'd all suddenly been told we had to turn up half an hour earlier in the mornings, regardless of what it said in our contracts; we were watched like hawks at lunchtimes, to check we weren't taking a minute more than our allotted hour; and instead of being a person who was readily approachable, whatever the problem one might have, he became about the last person one would dream of telling anything if one could avoid it.

My doctor had advised me to make it clear when telling my employer I was pregnant that I was not to be put under any stress. Since twin pregnancies are always more exhausting than single ones, and since I'd already miscarried one twin, I had to be especially careful not to overdo things. I duly told my boss all of this when I was three months pregnant, and we also discussed when I would be leaving. Though he seemed to accept my doctor's recommendation, I couldn't help noticing when I told him the date the birth was due that he charmingly wrote in his diary 'Rona drops 17 October'. I suppose that should have warned me what was in store. Over the next few weeks I had to put up with sly jokes about the pregnancy, and, far from helping me to take things easy, he started to nitpick about any time I had off. At this point I was still suffering the common symptoms of early pregnancy – nausea and a crushing fatigue – and on many days I was effectively dragging myself into work. But I've never been someone to take much time off for anything, and I did my best to carry on as normal. However, one day, returning to the office from lunch in town, I suddenly fainted in the street. When I came round, I took myself straight home to bed and called work to say I'd be off sick that afternoon. A couple of days later my boss came into my office and said, almost casually, that it would be nice to know in advance when I was going to be fainting and going off sick, since things at work had to be planned for. At the time I controlled my temper, but I was pretty cut up about it, and I guess the fuse for the eventual explosion between us was laid then.

All it needed was one more incident to spark it off, and, inevitably, that wasn't long in coming.

We had a cheese and wine do planned for some important clients one Friday afternoon. I'd been feeling sick all that week, struggling in on the Monday and Tuesday before ringing my doctor on Wednesday. He told me to stay in bed and rest as much as possible, which I duly did until Friday morning, when I made a mammoth effort and forced myself into the office, feeling like death, but anxious to make sure all was ready for the afternoon. When I got into work my boss and I had a tremendous row, after which I collapsed in tears. A friend drove me home. When Mark saw the state of me and heard what had happened, he was furious, so angry that if he could have got at him, he'd have ripped my boss from head to toe. As it was, I was already so upset I couldn't face any more trouble, and somehow managed to calm Mark down before ringing my doctor to tell him the whole story. He, too, was incensed, and said that under no circumstances was I to be subjected to such treatment, or more stress, and if there were any more problems he'd sign me off work for the duration of the pregnancy. He wrote a letter to my employer, and after that, in the last weeks before my wedding, my boss eased up on me to the extent that we either just made freezingly cold 'polite' conversation or ignored each other completely. It was hardly a happy working relationship, but at least it was better than being inquisitioned about every single minute I spent out of the office.

All that kept me going through those awful weeks was Mark, and our growing baby, and the prospect of the wedding. As usual, in the course of all the preparations, Mark and I both had surprises in store for each other. Even though we'd now been together for about eight months, I'd never actually revealed to Mark how old I was – and that I was almost six years older than him. Of course, he'd asked me outright, since he knew I was a bit older, but I'd fobbed him off with the adage that 'a lady never tells her age'. There wasn't any compelling reason why I hadn't told him; it was just that I felt a touch bothered about how he'd feel about what, on paper, looked like quite an age gap. So it was only when we discussed our marriage plans with the minister that the Awful Truth came out. The minister had to fill in a form with various routine information about us. After obtaining Mark's details, he then turned to me and asked my date of birth. Mark claims that at this point I looked across at him with an expression of horror and shock, before mumbling something inaudible. He was unable to resist the temptation to wind me up by saying loudly, 'Sorry? What was that?' Needless to say, my age made no difference to him whatsoever – other than giving him the chance to tease me about hiding it.

Mark's surprise for me was a sartorial one. Naturally, as I was much preoccupied with choosing my wedding dress, I asked him (as it were, casually) what *he'd* be wearing at the church. To my dismay, he replied that he'd be sporting a grey morning suit, top hat, and all the rest of it. I'd secretly been cherishing hopes that he'd want to wear a kilt, and tried to suggest it.

'No, no,' he said. 'In my part of the world, it's traditional to wear a morning suit. Just because I'm in Scotland, it doesn't mean I have to do as the Scots do.'

'Aye, but you've a Scottish father,' I urged.

But it was fruitless. I couldn't persuade him. My visions of this tall, well-built, fine man waiting for me at the altar in the traditional tartan seemed doomed never to materialize, especially when, after I'd been dropping hints almost every day, Mark turned to me and told me in no uncertain terms to drop the subject, he was *not* getting married in a kilt, and that was final!

By the time the day came, I was more or less reconciled to seeing him in a morning suit, and it was hardly uppermost in my mind as I made my way into the church on my father's arm. As I glanced up the aisle to where Mark stood, I practically stopped dead. For there he was in the full regalia: black velvet Prince Charlie jacket, white wing collar, black bow tie . . . and, of course, the kilt! I could hardly believe my eyes. He looked magnificent, and my face must have shone with delight. Mark says I mouthed something at him, he reckons probably a mild obscenity for having fooled me for so long, but all I remember thinking is how lovely he was. In fact all through the service I was so happy, I had trouble taming the tears that were trembling at the corners of my eyes. We had just the traditional marriage service, with one or two of our favourite hymns, in a quaint old church just large enough to accommodate the fifty or so friends and family we'd invited. But somehow the very simplicity of everything made it, for me, all the more moving. Truly I felt it set the seal on our relationship. In all my life since then, I've only once experienced a happiness to touch the joy I felt that day.

The reception was held at an ancient, beautiful hotel, granite-built and turreted like a castle, in an enormous hall framed entirely in carved oak. We all enjoyed ourselves tremendously, and I managed to provide everyone with some inadvertent entertainment by making a complete fool of myself when it came to cutting the cake.

The toastmaster had rallied everybody round and announced, 'Ladies and Gentlemen, may I have your attention please. The bride and bridegroom are about to cut the cake, so if you'd all like to get your cameras ready . . .' Everyone was sitting down, all prim and proper, watching. I went to stand up, and the toastmaster removed my chair so we would make an uncluttered picture. But in standing up, I caught the hem of my dress in the heel of my shoe, so I sat down again to disentangle it . . . on a non-existent chair. I bumped with a marked lack of ladylike grace on to the floor, where for a moment I lay flat on my back with my legs in the air and my dress frothing round me in a sea of satin and voile.

There was a dreadful hush, and everything was still for a second, as if we were indeed on camera and had been caught in a freeze-frame. I scrambled to my feet, scarlet with embarrassment, wondering what on earth I was going to do. Then I thought, 'Och, to pot!' and started to laugh. It was the only thing to do. As soon as I laughed, so did everyone else, and it became one of the talking points of the day – how Rona was under the table at her own wedding reception!

The rest of the festivities passed off without incident. In the evening, Mark and I were waved off on our honeymoon by the guests – as they thought, to spend the night elsewhere.

Unbeknown to them, we actually returned to the hotel via a long and winding back way, sneaking in through an authentically creaking oak door before climbing a tiny, tiny stone staircase to the bridal suite, where we were able to listen to the party going on below well into the wee hours.

The following morning at six o'clock, we drove to the airport to fly to Lanzarote in the Canary Islands for a week's honeymoon. In spite of having barely slept a wink because of the previous night's jollities, we were full of beans, excited about going abroad, and especially looking forward to starting our married life together. By this time I had passed the stage of feeling nauseous and tired, and felt physically and emotionally on top of the world, relaxed, full of new energy and delight in my pregnancy. I'd been for a second scan just three days before the wedding, which had shown that the baby was growing well and was perfectly formed. This time, Mark had been there too, so he'd had the chance to see our child at last and marvel at the miracle of it all. We'd both found the scan very reassuring, for we now knew that in spite of the early miscarriage and all the stress of the past weeks, our baby was fine. The hospital staff also hinted that perhaps I'd got my dates wrong and the pregnancy was further advanced than I'd thought – about twenty-one weeks, rather than nineteen or twenty. I knew this meant I was now well past the danger time for miscarriages, and nothing more could go wrong. Up until then I'd been cautiously resisting the urge to buy up the whole of Mothercare, and had restricted myself to windowshopping: now I allowed myself to buy one small sleepsuit. We planned to go on a major spree once we returned from honeymoon.

As we set off for the sun on that first married morning, we were both exhilarated. Recently, I'd felt small flutterings in my tummy. Though so faint and far inside me, I was sure it was the baby moving about, and it made the child even more real to me. The little being I'd first seen two months before was quickening, growing and stirring in its secret world. Only four months to go! We could hardly wait for October, when we would meet our baby for the very first time.

2
LOSS

We flew home from our honeymoon on a Thursday in late May. The week away had been simply wonderful, even though as a place, Lanzarote hardly made us leap up and down with excitement. Being a volcanic island, it had spectacular, if rather bizarre scenery: great black spires of hardened lava rising into the brilliant blue sky, and slabs of black rock, interspersed with black sand, layering the shores. In places, attempts had been made to create more inviting beaches by pouring shelves of imported silver sand over the black. But this dramatic appearance concealed a disappointingly dull inner life. As far as we were able to discover in such a short time, there wasn't much to do on the island apart from sitting by the pool and basking in the sun. The nightlife seemed restricted to repeat visits to the same bars, the same discos . . . and the same people.

However, none of this bothered us much. For we might as well have been off on another island of our own, an island of complete happiness. We were quite content to lie in the scorching sun all day, idly slipping in and out of the swimming pool; and at the risk of sounding perilously soppy, we both felt we could have spent weeks just lying in bed, gazing into each other's eyes and feeding one another grapes. In a way which is hard to define, being married had changed our lives immeasurably for the better.

And the baby seemed to have decided to join in the fun, too. On our very first evening away, as we sat relaxing on the hotel veranda after the flight, enjoying the last of the day's sunshine, I'd felt the first distinct movement, a faint but now unmistakable patter, in my tummy. I sprang to my feet crying excitedly, 'Mark! Mark! Come here quickly! She just kicked! She just kicked!' (For some reason, I'd always

15

thought of the baby as being a girl.) Unfortunately, he didn't manage to catch her kicking then, even though he sat beside me for ages with his hand on my stomach, hoping for the next move – much to the delight of a passing waiter, who took one look at us and exclaimed knowingly, 'Ah, bambino, bambino!'

As well as feeling the baby move, I also suddenly began to look convincingly pregnant during this week. In my case the transformation was quite startling. Literally overnight, my barely discernible bump popped out by about four inches, and none of the clothes I'd brought with me fitted any more. Now I looked, as well as felt, blooming.

The journey back was uneventful, though as usual, I felt airsick – looking back, I think the nausea was maybe slightly worse than on other flights, but not alarmingly bad. At the time, I didn't think much of it, and it passed once we were on the ground. We spent that night at my aunt's before travelling home early the next morning, as Mark was due to work that afternoon. Arriving back at the flat was lovely, for it was still full of cards, presents and balloons from the wedding, and a sense of celebration lingered on to greet our return.

Mark was on standby duty that weekend, which meant he could be called away to work at any moment, so we intended as usual to have a bit of a lie-in on Saturday morning, knowing we might not have that much time together over the next couple of days. However, I woke early with a nagging, period-type pain in the small of my back and some pain in my thighs. This went on for a while, so when Mark woke up I asked him to massage my back a little to see if this would relieve the cramps at all. But the pain persisted, and then I began to leak a bit of fluid, which concerned me. I instinctively thought, 'There's something wrong,' and my fears were fuelled when, while Mark was making the tea, I turned to the back of one of my pregnancy books to find symptoms similar to mine listed under 'Inevitable abortion/miscarriage'. I didn't tell Mark this, as I still hoped I was just being paranoid: but we agreed it would be best to ring the doctor anyway, just to be on the safe side.

The doctor was reassuring, and told me not to worry, it was probably only a urine infection, but it would be best to have a test to make sure. Since the surgery didn't have the facilities to do the appropriate test, he advised me to go to the hospital straight away, and said he'd ring to inform them I was coming. I was a bit disconcerted and, in my heart of hearts, very worried, but I tried to keep telling myself it was only a routine test and probably nothing to panic about. I dressed, kissed Mark goodbye, said I'd be back in about half an hour, and drove to the hospital.

I stayed alone in the waiting room for a few minutes. Somehow the actions of getting up, dressing, and coming into hospital seemed to have made the pain triple in intensity, and I now found I had to sit doubled up. There was no denying it; I couldn't pretend *this* was my imagination. And surely a urine infection couldn't cause such agony? I suddenly thought, 'What the hell's happening to me? Please God, don't let anything go wrong . . .' Fear began to clutch at my heart. I longed for Mark's comforting presence.

Soon I was ushered through into a single room on the antenatal ward. A nurse came in and asked, 'Do you want a pad?'

I looked at her wildly, before stammering, 'No, no . . . I don't think I need one.'

She nodded. 'Okay. The doctor will be with you shortly.' And then she was gone.

The pain ground on. Panic surged through me in tidal waves until I felt I must be engulfed, borne away. But no: it seemed I could actually sit there, quite still, and *must* sit; and sit I did, for what seemed an eternity, so lonely and frightened I felt like a lost child who knows there is no safety left in the world.

At last I heard the click of footsteps in the corridor. The doctor came in.

'Now, could you tell me exactly how you feel, and what your symptoms are, please?'

17

He listened carefully to my reply. 'Right. Any fetal move-ments from the baby this morning?'

My heart missed another beat. 'No . . . Well I can't feel any sensations clearly because of the pain in my back.'

'Not to worry. Now I'm going to do a test to see if your waters have broken.'

He proceeded to perform the test, which to my relief seemed to give a negative result.

But my relief was short-lived. I'll never forget the look on that doctor's face after he'd examined me – or his first words.

'I'm afraid, Mrs Walker, this doesn't look good. Although the test is telling me your waters haven't broken, I can actually see the amniotic sac which holds the baby.'

I struggled to understand what he had said, and stammered out, 'What . . . what do you mean "It doesn't look very good"? What's happening?'

'Well, the situation is that I can physically see the sac containing the baby . . . This means your cervix has started to dilate. It looks as if you're in labour.'

He added that he wanted to double-check, however, and went away to fetch some more equipment.

For a while, I was alone, with only his words echoing through my head in the deserted room. I felt completely numb, as if frozen to the bone. Then it was as if a deadly sickness passed through my whole body. I lay on the bed with my head turned towards the window, looking out at the trees. I watched the leaves stir and shiver in the wind as they always did, the ordinary clouds driven in tatters across the empty sky, and I knew I must be dreaming. Half an hour ago I'd been lying in my own warm bed with Mark, living our lives, content, happy. Now I lay in a strange solitary hospital room, in pain and very possibly in labour. The change was too sudden: I couldn't grasp it. It made no sense. I felt as if my life had been chopped in half, it was as if someone had taken a knife and just chopped something off. My head reeled from the blow; my stomach swilled and heaved, and I could feel terror rising in my throat like vomit until I thought I would actually be sick there on the floor.

I tried to latch on to the other world, that normal everyday life I'd had before the doctor spoke and smashed it to smithereens with one sentence – the real world that I could see through the window. It seemed at once very far and yet so near, as if only the pane of glass stood between me and normality. Surely I could go back there? I denied the doctor's words that spooled incessantly through my head, the bitter bile of panic in my mouth. I thought, 'No, no, this is not reality.' I was sure that soon someone would come and prod me awake, and we would laugh about these things as one tries to cast out bad dreams.

This sense of disbelief was very strong, and continued all through my time in hospital, especially on that first day, even as I was sucked into the horrible spiral of events. Yet alongside it came a growing realization of the disaster in which I was now caught up. With the part of me that understood what was happening I suddenly wanted someone to get hold of Mark right away, before he was called to work and out flying where no-one could reach him. When the nurse returned to see how I was, I told her this and she promised to deal with it at once.

The doctor returned and repeated the test. This time, it showed the waters *had* broken, as he thought. I asked him what would happen and what could be done. He explained that I was in fact in labour and it seemed inevitable that I would lose the baby. However, he added, very occasionally they had been known to be wrong about such cases, and that they would now try to stop labour progressing. Though he spoke very kindly and carefully, I understood there was little hope. I frantically searched my mind for a reason, something to explain how this could have happened: there had been nothing to trigger the labour off, for I'd been relaxing all the previous week, and had been quietly asleep when the pains started. I asked the doctor whether the fact of my earlier miscarriage might somehow have led to this one. He said no. Helplessly, I began to cry, and at the same time my mind went into fast-forward and I had to ask, 'Does this mean I won't be able to have another child?'

He said 'No, no, there's no reason at all why you shouldn't have another baby, don't you worry.'

This was a slight consolation, a gleam of hope. Another was brought by the nurse who came to explain what they were going to do next. 'Now Rona, we're going to take you through to the labour ward to see if we can stop your contractions. Don't you worry, dear. We've had ladies in before with the same sort of trouble, and they've been fine; we've stopped the labour, kept them in till twenty-eight weeks or so, and then delivered the babies and nursed them through. Now you'll maybe be the same. Don't you give up hope.'

My spirits rose a little at this, particularly as by this time Mark had joined me, and was holding my hand reassuringly. They took us through to a private room off one of the labour wards, and put me on a bed, the foot of which was then raised, so that I lay on a slant. This took any downward pressure off the uterus, and might therefore help lessen the contractions. At this stage, I still experienced these as a continuous grinding pain, mainly in my back, but it wasn't so fierce that I couldn't speak quite normally or concentrate on what was happening around me. A drip containing Ritodrine, a drug which could halt the contractions, was inserted into my arm. Mark sat down beside me, holding my hand, and a midwife joined us, placing her hand on my stomach most of the time, to see if labour let up at any point.

And so we sat, in our quiet but uneasy vigil, as the hours went by and the afternoon wore on: and nothing happened. In spite of the drip, the contractions continued, neither gathering nor lessening in intensity. For some unknown reason, the labour seemed to be static: my cervix wasn't dilating any further, yet all attempts to stop the contractions failed. Eventually, towards evening, the doctor came and advised us that it would be dangerous for me to continue in this way any longer. Since my cervix was open and the waters had ruptured, there was a risk that I would contract an ascending infection. The only real option was for labour to be accelerated artificially. I would now have to deliver the baby.

I said to the doctor, 'You mean I'm actually going to give birth now?'

'Yes.'

Through my terror, I again experienced a tremendous sense of disbelief, I thought, 'This is a dream, I'm going to wake up in the morning and it will all be over.' I looked at the doctor, his calm, matter-of-fact expression, which seemed to imply this was an unquestionable, routine event. I was incredulous. I thought wildly, 'This guy's an idiot, he doesn't know what he's talking about!'

But at the same time half of me obviously understood the reality, for I felt a fresh wave of panic rise and batter me at the prospect of going into full labour. I felt I wasn't ready, either physically or mentally. In a normal pregnancy, a woman has nine months in which to prepare herself for the birth: she has a good while in which to accustom herself gradually to the idea, grasp its reality as far as she can, and gather her strength for the event. Most of this was denied me. At about twenty-two weeks pregnant, I already knew all about childbirth in theory – I'd read everything about it I could lay my hands on. And in theory, I was looking forward to it, it was something I very much wanted to do, to experience. But because I was only halfway through my pregnancy, I hadn't started my course of childbirth classes, and I hadn't yet geared myself up fully, emotionally, for the birth. This morning I'd been happily thinking about the months ahead, just starting to plan the decor for the baby's room, and what to buy for the layette. Now I was facing the prospect of actually delivering within a matter of hours. I was terrified.

I clasped Mark's hand, and he squeezed mine hard, try-ing to reassure me. I looked to him, feeling so hurt and vulnerable, crying silently to him with my eyes to help me, help me. The doctor explained to us what they would do, and then, as if he'd flicked a switch, the inexorable clinical procedure of induction began, in a chilly silence punctuated only by the brisk brief sounds of standard practice; a sharp scrape of metal, a buzz of electrics. There was a dull thud as they lowered the bed to the normal level. The first drip was removed, and a new one, containing oxytocin, a hormone which stimulates contractions, was inserted into my other arm. Soon the persistent nagging in my back was transformed into distinct contractions which took on a definite pattern, each one starting fairly mildly, building to a height, then fading away before the next began.

Quite how long this lasted I don't know – Mark and I both lost track of time as we were so involved in the labour. The contractions were soon strong enough for me to need gas and air to cope with the pain, and Mark was busy helping me to breathe deeply and relax my shoulders. Over the next few hours people kept coming in to do various checks and tests; at one point, I remember, they tried to increase dilatation of the cervix by using a prostaglandin gel. For even now, in spite of strong contractions, the cervix wasn't opening any further, so the baby couldn't be pushed down into the birth canal to be born. Again, labour seemed to have stuck fast, and for all my pain and my body's internal efforts, nothing was happening.

Around eight o'clock that evening, after I'd been examined several times, we were advised that, inexplicably, the cervix wasn't dilating any further, and if they left me in this state much longer there was a risk of infection which might endanger my life. They said there was no alternative but to take me into the operating theatre: they would then try to deliver the baby vaginally by hand, under a general anaesthetic, or, failing that, they would have to do a Caesarean.

This had to be the worst moment of the whole experience so far. I had been frightened enough at the idea of going into labour, but this was far, far worse. I desperately didn't want to go into that operating theatre. The idea of being unconscious, out of control, while they delivered my baby simply petrified me. My immediate reaction was to protest. I blurted out that I didn't want a Caesarean, I wanted to do this on my own, I'd get down on the floor, or walk about, or squat, or do anything rather than have to submit to that; I *couldn't* go into the operating theatre.

But I was clutching at straws. The staff were sympathetic,

but stressed that unless this was done, my life could be in danger. There was no choice.

I think the whole thing was harder to bear because I felt more or less fine, or as fine as one can feel in labour, so I couldn't easily accept the business of my life being at risk; it had no real meaning for me. On top of this I now had to face the fact that I was going to lose the baby. It will sound very strange, but until then it hadn't crossed my mind, not seriously, that we might lose her, or that she might already be dead. Rationally, I knew how young she was, how slim the chances of survival were: yet while she was still inside me, though I'd been in labour for hours, it didn't really enter my head that we would actually lose her. I suppose all along I'd felt this disbelief at what was happening; I was also very tired, and in quite a lot of physical pain, which clouded my mind a little. Above all, I'd suffered a series of shocks since early that morning, with each new turn of events proving worse than the last, and perhaps I just couldn't deal with all of it at once, so I'd blanked out the thought of losing the baby, and somehow refused to accept it. Certainly, neither of us remembers anyone mentioning the baby all through this time, and I was never monitored to check the fetal heartbeat. Maybe the staff assumed the baby was already dead: whereas Mark and I assumed, I think, that somehow she might be saved. I don't know.

In any case, I knew then that I would be going into that operating theatre specifically because they were going to remove the baby, to take her out of my body. She would be taken from me while I couldn't actually see or do anything about it. A sense of helplessness and loss came over me: it was such a draining feeling, as if someone had just come along and said, 'Well, that's it, you've had all the good luck you're going to have. That's you finished now.' It was a horrible feeling, almost like a kind of sickness; horrible, horrible, horrible.

They started to prepare me for the operation. I knew from having previously had a dental operation that I was allergic to the premed injection, which helps to relax you before you go under the full anaesthetic, so they said they'd have to leave that and take me to theatre completely awake. I was told to take off all my jewellery – my necklace, my rings.

This was a bad moment. The simple routine actions somehow brought everything home to me. Mark and I were going to be parted; now, when I needed him more than ever, I was going to have to go into that strange place on my own, and who knew then what would happen, or when we would see each other again?

I removed the little gold treble clef I'd worn as a pendant and my wedding ring and threaded them together on the chain which Mark fastened round his neck. I was then helped on to a trolley. As I lay down I caught sight of Mark's face watching me. Every single dot of colour was gone from it, he looked just like a ghost. Typically, he was trying to smile at me – *for* me – but his eyes told such a sad story. He looked so vulnerable, all I wanted to do was reach out and give him a hug, but the pain prevented me from moving.

I watched his face all the way to the operating theatre. He held my hand in his own strong clasp. That short walk was a very cold and scary experience; my mind churned with fear. Fear of the unknown; of the operation; of going in with a baby inside me, and coming out with her gone. At the doors the nurse stopped the trolley briefly so Mark and I could say goodbye. I don't remember exactly what we said. I think Mark tried to say something witty to cheer me, but the look on his face wiped any humour from his words. It was as much as I could do to let go of his hand. Then I was wheeled alone through the swing doors and into the operating theatre.

Inside, it was a large white-and-green space, efficiently gleaming with equipment and hung with huge overhead lamps. I'm sure it actually was warm, but I felt chilled and empty, and afraid. I could only think, 'Please, please hurry up and put me to sleep.' There seemed to be about five or six people there, including an anaesthetist who immediately came over to administer the injection. I tried not to look much at anything around me, for this only made things worse. When they took my arm I shivered with fear, for

24

just this simple movement filled me with a consuming panic. Someone was speaking to me all the while, but the only words I remember were from a disembodied voice saying, 'You'll be off in a minute. You'll wake up in the morning and it'll all be over.' Something, or someone, touched my head, perhaps putting a hat on to keep my hair out of the way, perhaps just laying a hand on my brow to soothe me, I don't recall. I thought of Mark, and how badly I needed him. I thought of the looming lights above me, and the strange space around me, and in those last seconds before the anaesthetic took hold I felt sheer terror.

They say a drowning person rises three times to the surface before sinking for the last and fatal time. My only memories of the next hours are of swimming up briefly and repeatedly from unconsciousness before plunging back into sleep.

None of these awakenings were happy experiences – though luckily, I stayed conscious the third time – but the first was the worst. I woke up, thinking dimly that the operation was over. But for some reason I was still in the theatre. My head was thumping, the room was spinning, and I was being violently sick, retching and retching as if poisoned, till it felt as if all I could have left to bring up were my own guts. The sickness was so bad I couldn't tell if I were alive or dead, but it did seem to me I must be dying. I could also feel a strong pulsing pressure, together with wetness, between my legs. I couldn't see anything, I could only hear the sharp clinking of instruments on a stainless steel tray; a disgusting sucking sound from the pipe that was draining vomit from my throat; and, as if in the distance, the small noises of people scuttering about. I gasped for air as the sickness shook me. I felt I was choking, and that this was it, the end of my life had come, and I cried out, 'Mark, Mark, please help me!' Then the sickness, the sounds, everything spiralled away as I was once more dragged under into unconsciousness.

When I next came to, I seemed to be being wheeled into another room – though I was only semi-conscious, and didn't open my eyes. Some of the dreadful nausea still lingered, and I felt as if I were stuck as full of needles as a hedgehog. There seemed to be needles everywhere: in my arms, my hands, my body. To make matters worse, somebody was – inexplicably to me – stabbing at my ankles with yet another syringe. Though I didn't know it, Mark was with me by now, and told me later what had happened. Apparently a young doctor had just decided she needed to take one more blood sample, and was trying to get it from the veins in my ankles, since they were some of the few left available! I knew nothing of this at the time, apart from the fact that I was feeling awful, uncomfortable and exhausted, and here was somebody treating my feet like pincushions. I wanted just to get up and walk away from the situation, but of course I couldn't move. I don't remember what I said, but Mark tells me I started kicking out, mumbling and muttering obscenities. Eventually, the doctor managed to get the wretched sample and left, only to be replaced by someone who started turning and flopping me over, and, as it seemed to me, pushing and poking me about. Mark told me later how they'd had to move me in order to take X-rays, and described the rather absurd sight of the tiny radiographer manoeuvring a great lumbering beast of an X-ray machine through the double doors, just managing to squeeze it into the room. I'm afraid the comic side of all this rather passed me by at the time: all I was aware of was a longing to be left alone, to lie still and go to sleep.

At last, all the tests and checks were done, and everyone seemed to fade away. All a-quiver with needles as I was, I did what hedgehogs do best and sank into a deep sleep like a hibernation.

Later, on the Sunday morning, I woke up feeling slightly more myself. The first thing I noticed was a violent pain in my stomach. The skin felt raw and stretched taut, and there seemed to be lumps and bumps all the way down, as if I'd been cut and then stitched. Glancing under the sheet, I saw to my dismay a long strip of surgical tape, covering a scar that seemed to run from the top of my belly button right down to my pubic bone. I immediately guessed that they'd done a Caesarean. I was thoroughly miserable: not just because of the Caesarean, which I'd always dreaded, but also because they'd made such a long vertical cut, for I'd hoped that if they had to do one they'd give me a neat, bikini-line scar. Before I could think any more about it, the doctors came in to see me.

'Good morning, Mrs Walker. How are you feeling?'

I answered without hesitation. 'Lousy.'

'Well, we're all absolutely amazed at your resilience. You've just come through a very, very long operation and you've had quite a bad time of it.'

I immediately asked, 'You had to do a Caesarean then?'

The doctor who'd spoken hesitated a little. Then he murmured, 'Mmm. Yes I'm sorry we didn't manage to make the scar as you would have wished.'

There was a small pause as I gathered myself to ask the next question that burned in my mind. I'd realized straight away when I woke that there was no baby with me in the room. 'Was it . . . was it a boy or a girl?' He told me it was a little girl, and that she was approximately twenty-two or twenty-three weeks, perfect in every way, but they were very sorry, she had already died by the time they delivered her. Again, there was a silence. Then, as there seemed nothing more to say, the doctors went away again.

This news itself was like a death, but at the time it struck me as simply the latest in a series of terrible events: another hope gone. I don't think I really took it in, not properly at any rate; I think I still wasn't quite myself, or I'd have asked at once where the baby was and if I could see her – as I now desperately wish I had. As it was, I was fairly groggy, and struggling with a tremendous amount of abdominal pain, and I think I must have been in shock from all that had hit me. At any rate, a nurse came in then to check on me; and Mark, who'd been asleep in a chair by my bed, woke up. He came over to me and took my hand.

I said 'The doctors have just been through, they told me what happened.'

I hardly noticed him glance across at the nurse, who at once withdrew, leaving us alone together.

Mark asked gently, 'What did they tell you?'

'Well, I've felt my scar. So . . . I had to have a Caesarean after all.'

Something faltered in his face. He seemed somehow at a loss; then, in a hoarse voice that strove to soften the blow, he said, 'No, Rona, they had to do more than that . . . They . . . had to do a hysterectomy.'

I registered the word, I knew what it meant, but I had to make my mind believe it, I had to insist, 'You mean they've actually taken out my womb?'

Helplessly, he nodded, and almost swallowed his one word.

'Yes.'

3
DARK DAYS

Why, why, why? The question broke out through the storm of crying that immediately overwhelmed me. I wept as if my heart would break; I felt utter desolation. It was such a wound. Not just to lose our baby before we had had a chance to know her, but to lose also any chance of ever bearing another child. How could this have happened, how could it?

The grief was unanswerable, but even through his own suffering, Mark did his best to provide me with at least some explanation of what had happened in the operating theatre. 'Doing a hysterectomy was the only way to save your life after they'd delivered the baby, you were losing so much blood. You . . . you almost lost your life, Rona, you were critically ill, I called your mum and Megan, they've been here waiting, and hoping . . . We're just so glad you're here now . . .'

The tension and pain of those past terrible hours coloured every word he spoke to me then, before he too broke down, and we cried in each other's arms. When the first wave of grief had washed through us both, he told me more of what had happened, and over the next couple of days I gradually began to piece the whole story together from his account and from what we were told by the consultant who'd performed the hysterectomy, Professor Churchill.

These, in outline at least, were the facts. Once I was under anaesthetic, the doctors had managed to deliver the baby vaginally by hand; that is, without surgery. Although the cervix hadn't fully dilated, the baby, being of only about twenty-two weeks' gestation, was small enough to enable them to remove her without too much difficulty. Though perfect in every way, she was already dead; they stressed

29

to me that she hadn't died because she was abnormal, or because of the operation, but only because labour had begun too soon.

Up until this point everything had gone as well as could be expected in the circumstances. The problems began as they were delivering the afterbirth, or placenta, which began to come away from the womb – as usual – as soon as the baby was born. However, instead of shearing away cleanly from the wall of the uterus, as it normally would, it tore, and I began to haemorrhage massively. The doctors tried everything to stop the bleeding, but nothing worked. I was now losing blood at such a rate that I was very near to cardiac arrest. Normally, there are about nine pints of blood circulating in your body at any one time; in all, I lost twenty-one, nineteen of them while actually on the operating table, as they tried frantically to pump more blood back into me. It was this tremendous blood loss that caused me to come round momentarily, mid-operation. As the blood poured out, it was very difficult to pump more in fast enough, so there came a point when there simply wasn't enough blood to hold the anaesthetic in my body. Because of the blood loss it was also very hard to judge how much fresh anaesthetic to administer – too much would have been fatal, and too little would have left me still semi-conscious.

At this stage, Mark, anxiously pacing the corridor outside, had heard me cry out faintly to him. Though he wondered if he'd imagined it, nevertheless it sent him cold. Moments later a doctor emerged from the theatre. As he came towards him Mark saw the look on his face and thought this was it, the doctor was going to tell him I had gone. Instead, he said they were very sorry, but they would have to perform a hysterectomy to save my life. Though the news shook Mark, he was so relieved I was still alive, he couldn't immediately take in the reality of what a hysterectomy meant.

In any case, there was no alternative. By this time, the top consultant at the hospital had been called into the theatre to perform a laparotomy – an investigative operation – to find out why I was haemorrhaging so badly. This suggested that I'd had what is known as a cervical implantation, a very rare occurrence in which instead of growing within the womb itself, the baby develops in the neck of the womb or the cervix, and the afterbirth embeds itself in the tissue there, which is covered in blood vessels. So, as my placenta came away from the cervix, this itself had torn. The result was like opening a valve, causing all the blood in my body to flood out. As soon as he discovered this, the consultant performed a hysterectomy – the only way, and with literally seconds to spare, to save me from death. He did literally that – saved my life – staff worked hours over their shifts to see me through the operation that one doctor described as a nightmare.

Professor Churchill also explained that because the baby had implanted in the cervix, this had been unable to dilate fully during labour, thus preventing a normal delivery.

So that was everything accounted for – the whole tragedy, step after disastrous step, seemed to have been explained, for the moment anyway. Later, both Mark and I were to ask many, many more questions about every stage of the experience, anxious, I suppose, to know for certain that it had all really been inevitable. I *do* know my life was saved, but it's so hard in the face of such events just to accept they've happened at all, that maybe it's a natural reaction to try to be sure there *was* no choice, that it *had* to happen as it did. I don't know. In any case, at the time, I think we were both still so numb from the shock that we didn't take in every detail; but it was a help to discuss it, and to begin at least to understand why things had gone so terribly wrong.

But it *was* only the beginning of what was to be a very long and dark time of coming to terms with everything. During the first few days in hospital I was in such physical pain that half the time my mind couldn't really get to grips with the loss. I suppose your mind thinks about the pain you're actually feeling physically, and then the full mental anguish comes later . . . The agonizing pain in my stomach meant that in spite of painkilling injections, I often couldn't sleep at night, and once or twice begged the nurses to give me an extra shot before the due time – but of course they couldn't as it was too dangerous. So I just had to get on with it as best I could.

31

Thankfully, I was rarely alone. Mark had compassionate leave, and was with me nearly all the time; day and night he stayed by my bedside, comforting me, soothing me, mustering smiles even though he'd had hardly any sleep for two or three days, and was very pale and drawn. Instinctively, I looked to him for strength, and somehow, though physically and emotionally exhausted himself, he always found more to give me.

Small things, little routines, also became very important to me in getting through each day. I soon had a roomful of well-wishing flowers, so many, they had to take them out at night, because of the oxygen. Every evening after dinner they took the vases away, one by one; and each morning I looked forward to the return of all those masses of colours, brightening up the room.

Apart from such little certainties, it was hard to look forward. For now there seemed no end to the blows that could fall. Only two days after the operation, Mark came back from a quick check on the flat and told me quietly that he'd just received news that his father had died the night before. Stunned by the trauma of the weekend, we found it very hard to take this in all at once. The main feeling I had when he told me was what have we done, why is this happening to us?

Although Mark's father had been terminally ill for some time, he'd borne his illness with such courage and so cheerfully that somehow we hadn't expected him to die: it seemed very sudden. For this to happen now, when we were already in such despair, for Mark not to be able to see his father again or talk to him about everything, seemed like a triple blow. He was quite close to his father, and I remember watching his poor, worn face and wondering how he would cope with this. I'd never seen him like this, he looked utterly empty and lost. I wanted so badly to take all the grief away. In the past day I'd started to understand just how much he'd suffered; while I'd been unconscious during the trauma of the operation, he'd been awake, cut off from me in that lonely corridor for hours, helplessly waiting for news. And now, just when he was trying to come to terms with what had happened, tragedy had struck again.

I think the only thing that kept him going was the fact he had to look after me, and in a couple of weeks I'd be coming out of hospital. Although Mark hardly said anything at that moment, I knew he was grieving deeply for his father in his own way. But he was numb with loss. He'd just lost his daughter, and almost lost his wife; to lose his father now was just too devastating for him to accept in such a short space of time, let alone express.

In any case, there was no need for him to speak openly to me in order for me to know how he was feeling. For our relationship had undergone an unparalleled deepening. It was as if our minds were talking to each other without a word actually being spoken. Mercifully, almost magically, mixed with the terrible sadness, pain and tears of that time, came the most tremendous feeling of love between us. A strange, intense joy sprang up, like something shining and pulsating deep inside – a wonderful, wonderful, silent closeness. The bond we had was now so strong, at times it was as if the rest of the world was shut out, so that although grief surrounded and poured through us, we still had, too, a deep core of happiness. It was like nothing I'd ever experienced before, and I know it gave me great strength through all those dark, tormented days and nights.

Without Mark, without that extraordinary love, I hate to think what I'd have done, because at times I just didn't want to go on. Up until the end of the first week in hospital I didn't exactly feel depressed: essentially that time was taken up with recuperating physically. But in the last three or four days of my stay acute depression set in. As my body began to heal, my mind took over and started working overtime: every waking moment I thought of nothing but those terrible events and I couldn't concentrate on anything except why, why, why this had happened. I felt worse as the time to leave drew nearer. For in hospital I felt very protected as it was a secure environment where I was cared for, where everybody knew what had happened to me, and we could talk about it whenever we wished. So in a way, I didn't want to leave:

I didn't want to get back to my 'normal' life. Too many things were still unresolved. I didn't really know *how* I was going to live. My mother had tried to comfort me by telling me, 'Life goes on,' but it seemed to me then that that was exactly what *hadn't* happened. Life hadn't gone on, life had just died, and part of me felt dead.

Part of me *was* dead, of course. I had asked about the baby straight away, as soon as I came round after the operation. Though I knew she was dead, and wouldn't look like a live, full-term baby, I wanted to see her, and maybe also to have a chance to hold her. But the staff advised against it, because they thought in my condition I wouldn't be able to cope with any more shock, any more grief. They said that because of the circumstances of her birth she had been put in formalin, a preserving solution, for the time being, but that photographs had been taken of her which would be put in with my medical notes, and I could look at these photos whenever I felt up to it. Even if it took ten years for me to decide to look at them, they would always be there for me to see, the nurses promised.

I wish now that I'd demanded to see the baby herself, then and there, for I know how important that need is for me, to have had the chance to look at her in the flesh, to acknowledge her, and to say farewell. But in those early days of loss I had only just begun to grieve, and the pain of it was all so sudden and so new to me, I didn't know then how much I needed that glimpse of her, or how never seeing her would torment me in the months and years to come. So I let it pass, thinking that at least some day I would see her photograph.

Even if I didn't see her, I still thought of her constantly. As my stay in hospital drew to an end, I was troubled by the fact that I didn't know where she was, or what would happen to her when I'd gone. For me, something had to be done about her body; I couldn't bear to think of her just drifting lifelessly away in some part of the hospital, or worse, never knowing at all what had been done with her. I had to lay her to rest. And I needed very badly to make something of her life, to express to her that Mark and I loved her; I suppose to say to her, 'You may not be here now but for us you are so real, you will always exist.'

We'd already decided to give her a name, because she was a human being, no matter how short her life was. Emma was the name we chose. On the morning I was due to leave, I told one of the nurses how upset I was about parting from Emma like this; I felt I was deserting her. The nurse asked if I would like to speak to the hospital chaplain, Rev. Swinton, because she knew that he might be able to arrange a service for the baby. As soon as she mentioned this, I felt greatly relieved and comforted, and said I would very much like to speak to the chaplain. Though he wasn't actually in the hospital that day, the nurse promised to find him and let him know that I needed to talk, and sure enough, he visited me soon after I came home.

He explained that, because no death certificate is signed for babies who die before the twenty-eighth week of pregnancy, their parents have no open acknowledgement of the baby's life and death, which makes it even harder to cope with losing the child. He knew this from personal experience, and so tried to help parents in such a situation by holding special cremation services for the babies about every three months, in order to commemorate their lives properly. He told us that at each service, the babies who had recently died in these circumstances were cremated together, and, if we wished, Emma could be included in the next one, which we could attend on 29 July. Rev. Swinton added that he would enquire about Emma's body at the hospital, and ensure she was actually cremated at the service, so it would be a true funeral for her.

We agreed that this was what we wished to do. Making these arrangements, talking about Emma with someone from 'outside' who completely understood how we felt, was a great help. We didn't want her to feel that simply because she didn't live she wasn't wanted, or wasn't cared for. In the rest of the life that lay ahead of me, I knew it might be hard to talk about her to other people, however much I might want to. It seemed almost inevitable that her life would gradually become shrouded in silence. But in the service at least we would be able to hear her spoken of, to think only of her, our daughter, and express our love for her and our aching grief at her little lost life.

I now somehow had to come to terms with another loss: the loss of my past self. Already, I knew I had changed. I felt odd, because I had no womb: I knew I was still a woman, of course, but in a way I felt abnormal now, not quite complete. Though I wasn't offered specific counselling about how to deal with this, or with losing Emma, while I was still in hospital one of the nurses, Sister Grant, gave me a lot of help, just by speaking very frankly about my position. In the last days before I left, she encouraged me to grieve whenever and for as long as I needed to. Days when I was having a particularly bad time, she'd come in and say, 'Look, Rona, I'm going to shut this door and put a sign on saying DO NOT DISTURB. You just sit there and cry your eyes out until you can't cry any more. Don't hold anything back, let it all out. Then I'll come back and give you a cup of tea, and we'll have another chat about everything.'

She also started to prepare me for returning to the outside world. She asked me if I understood that I would have to face people I knew, friends and so on, who wouldn't have heard what had happened and would ask about the baby; and also, people who *would* know, but who just wouldn't be able to handle the situation and who might try to avoid me, so I would probably lose some friends.

She also spelt out in black-and-white exactly what I had to face about my circumstances if I was going to be able to get on with my life. She said, 'You've got to accept that you're a changed person; you'll never be the same person that you were before you came in here. But you're not abnormal, just because you've had a hysterectomy. Lots of other women have hysterectomies, only they've maybe had their children by then; whereas you haven't had your children, and you wanted to have your children, and you'll never be able to have them. You'll maybe also have to deal with your family's disappointment. You'll never be able to give your mother, or your mother-in-law, grandchildren . . .'

Written down like this, these words may look very harsh and hurtful, but this wasn't how they were intended: though they did hurt, they were what I, personally, needed, and I think Sister Grant knew that. She was the only person to talk to me in this totally direct way about the reality of my situation, and this was a tremendous relief to me, especially as I prepared to leave the sanctuary of the hospital where I had lived for ten days. Though part of me wanted to go, to get home, another part of me wanted to stay; I was distraught at leaving my unseen, unknown baby, and I felt I still had so many questions I wanted to ask, questions that could only be answered there, where it had all happened. Perhaps I also felt I'd be leaving part of myself behind.

Inevitably, the day to leave came round. It was a lovely, sunny, windy day, one of those fresh days that blows the cobwebs away. Mark came to pick me up in the car; as we drove along I smelt the cool, bright air, and saw trees and green grass again for the first time in ten days. I suddenly felt exhilarated – in fact I opened the car window and half-froze us both to death.

Coming into the flat was good, too: the cards and presents from the wedding were still around, vivid reminders of happiness.

In the first week home, also, everything seemed to go well, because Mark was off work. But once he went back, life took a turn for the worse. I was alone a lot of the time, and my thoughts came crowding round inexorably. They were always the same: that constant, unanswerable, grieving question, Why? – and Emma, and what had happened. There wasn't a day, not a day, that I didn't think about her. It was to be months before she, and the whole experience, stopped being the first things on my mind when I woke up in the morning; and in those first weeks and months they occupied about ninety percent of my waking life. It didn't matter what I was doing outwardly: I'd be talking to Mark about something else, or watching television, while inside, my mind would be churning over and over the events leading up to the hospital, the time in the hospital and since – and why, why, why?

Sometimes the thoughts carried on into my troubled sleep. People say sleep can be healing, and in some of my dreams my mind seemed to be trying to mend things for me, by going over the story, but changing it in crucial ways. Soon after coming home I had a dream in which I was back in the hospital, in labour, but I absolutely refused to go to the operating theatre, insisting that I was going to deliver the baby myself – which I did, giving birth in the normal way, as I'd always wanted to. Then they handed the baby to me to hold. In that mysterious way of dreams, though nobody said so, we knew she wasn't going to live more than a few moments, but we sat there and held her, and looked at her together until she died. This dream recurred in exactly the same form about three or four times over the next six months. I always woke from it crying and sweating, as if I had actually lived through in reality the events it described.

During this period I seemed to have entered limboland. I felt as if I was bound forever to go over and over the same track, never being free of these shadows. I tried to put a brave face on it most of the time. I usually only cried after Mark had gone out to work, because I didn't want to make him feel worse by showing him that I really was much worse than I might seem to be. Though I almost immediately started to try and do something positive about the situation, alongside all this activity, or underneath it, I was still often in the depths of depression. I know now that this was all part of the grieving process, and that even today, while the depression has lifted and there is so much in my life to be glad about, the loss of Emma will always be unresolved to some extent, and there'll always be a ghost there. But I don't ever want to forget her, because she's very much a part of us, and she's gone; and how our life has changed since losing her matters a great deal to me. It's through her I've discovered how strangely events that seem like beginnings can be endings; and endings, too, can be beginnings. Until everything went wrong, I'd imagined Emma's birth as the start of a new life, and a new phase in *our* lives; yet it proved to be the end of part of my life, and of hers. But in another way, losing her was also the start of another path, a fresh determination in our lives. For it was through our love and grief for her that we set out on our lonely, difficult quest to somehow have another child.

4

THE SEARCH

I began thinking about ways I could have children while I was still in hospital, recovering from the operation. This may seem a bit shocking, as if hardly had I learnt of Emma's death than my mind turned to having a second baby. But all I can say is that great grief and loss affect people in various ways, and it was hard for me initially to admit what had happened. Even as I struggled to face it and fully express my pain, I felt I just had to get on and do something: the only way even to begin to get to grips with losing Emma and with having had a hysterectomy was to concentrate on having another child as soon as possible. I knew that I could never 'replace' her, for she was special, a unique person. But I desperately needed a baby, I felt an almost overwhelming maternal urge which only a tiny child could satisfy. I knew that otherwise I'd always feel this longing, this hankering in my heart, and my life could never be fulfilled.

Professor Churchill, the consultant, had told me that though I no longer had a womb, I still had my ovaries intact and would have the same normal hormone balances as other women. When I heard this, I immediately began considering what I then thought of as 'surrogacy'. What I had in mind at this point – though I didn't know all the different terms at the time – was what's actually called 'host mothering', or 'host surrogacy'. This is where the biological mother's egg and the biological father's sperm are fertilized together in a test tube, using *in vitro* fertilization (IVF) techniques, and the fertilized egg is then implanted in the womb of a 'host' – a woman who's prepared to carry and give birth to the child, but who has no genetic relation to it. As one woman has rather aptly put it, the host acts as a kind of 'hotel' for the growing foetus for nine months.

At this stage I was completely ignorant of the existence of the other form of surrogacy, whereby the child is conceived by inseminating the surrogate mother with the sperm of the father, so that genetically, the surrogate is the child's mother, but she gives the baby up to the so-called 'commissioning' couple – the father and his wife – after the birth. All my queries to the doctors at the hospital were about host mothering, and nobody said anything about this other kind of surrogacy at the time. I was told that, in theory, what I wanted to do was medically possible, but the doctors warned me that I would have difficulty finding a host, as I wasn't allowed to advertise for one. This had been made illegal by the 1985 Surrogacy Arrangements Act, which also made it very difficult for any doctor to assist us; the Act prohibits a third party from assisting in such practices for commercial gain, and its terms are so vague that many doctors are fearful of involvement in any form of surrogacy in case the law might be interpreted in a way that would lead to prosecution.

Though I saw that host surrogacy would be very difficult and probably very expensive, I didn't fully understand in those early weeks that what we wanted to do was a definite no-go. I came out of hospital thinking that some day, somehow, medical science would help us to have our own genetic child. Seeking more information, I went and discussed it with my GP. He told me to take things easy, not to start thinking about this yet, not to start thinking about anything, in fact: he said I'd need some time to recover before looking into these things. He was echoing the advice of the nurses at the hospital, who'd said I should make time to be at home, at peace, before doing anything, or rushing into projects while my emotions were still in turmoil. Perhaps they all knew how difficult it would be trying to have another child, and wanted to save me from any more disappointment and distress. But being the person that I am, I couldn't take this advice. I had to find something to concentrate on, something positive that would help me look forward.

When my initial enquiries about host surrogacy came to what seemed like a dead end, I turned my attention to adoption. I have to admit that at this time, I would rather have had our own genetic child, because I felt very strongly that only another baby of *ours* could begin to fill the terrible void where Emma had been. But host surrogacy was beginning to look like a dream – something I knew happened in the United States, but that no one had achieved over here. I didn't completely give up this dream, but if I was going to do something constructive right away, adoption now seemed the most obvious course.

I threw myself into this search with a vengeance. As far as I was concerned, we were perfectly suitable and there wouldn't be any reason why we couldn't adopt a baby; my hopes were high, partly because Professor Churchill had suggested that perhaps the adoption agencies might consider our case more favourably because of our particular circumstances. In June, immediately after coming out of hospital, I set about writing to all the adoption organizations. I was told to contact our local authority once I had the relevant papers, and wasted no time in doing just that.

Then came the first shock. The authority informed me that due to overwhelming demand, the list for our district had been closed for two years, would probably remain closed for about another year, and that there was a waiting period of approximately four years after that before a baby might become available to us. I was stunned – I'd no idea of the demand for adoptive babies, nor that there were now so very few around. The authority tried to be helpful: I was offered an appointment for some time within the next six months, just before the list was due to open again, to discuss the adoption procedure. However, I asked whether they could give me any information now, at once, about our chances, and told them what our position was. This brought on another big shock. The authority told me that age was a significant factor in deciding on a couple's suitability as adoptive parents, and that my age would count against us. I was already thirty-two, and the cut-off point set by the authority was thirty-five. By the time a baby became available, and we had been assessed, I would almost certainly be too old.

Still clutching at straws, I wrote to, or telephoned, every single local authority in the United Kingdom. It transpired that on this issue at least, the authorities of the kingdom were indeed united. Everywhere I tried, I met with the same response. There was sympathy for our predicament, but it was explained to me quite clearly that there wasn't much hope of our ever being able to adopt a baby under the present circumstances. It was also made plain – rather brusquely plain – that it was up to us to try to tailor our needs to match those of the children who were available, and not the other way round. Indeed I was told in no uncertain terms by a woman at one of the adoption agencies that we would have to 'lower our standards'.

I'd phoned her totally cold, without knowing anything much about adoption – I was very green then. As soon as I mentioned that we'd like to adopt a baby, she exclaimed, 'A baby!? What do you mean by a *baby*?!'

When I tried to explain what had happened, she wasn't interested, and more or less threw up her hands in horror at the very idea that we could even *hope* to be offered a young baby – evidently, that was out of the question.

Her response did me a lot of damage. I felt completely undermined, humiliated almost, as if I were a fool to be even thinking of such a thing. The only glimmer of hope I was offered was that we might get a child if we would consider adopting either a special needs baby, or an older one. We thought about this a great deal, but after much heart-searching concluded that we just couldn't meet the demands of a special needs child; we didn't think we had that kind of strength. Nor could I see my way to adopting an older child. I felt such a tremendous need to nurture a little baby like the one I had lost; it wasn't as if I'd had a long history of infertility, and had therefore never expected to have a baby. I'd actually *had* my own baby, whom I had lost without ever seeing in the flesh. I felt that with an older child, I'd always be pining for the baby stage I'd never had. For this reason I felt perhaps I wouldn't be able to love an older child in the way I'd love a baby, and that this wasn't a good basis on which to adopt.

As a last resort, I contacted the National Association of the Childless (NAC). The response was very sympathetic . . .

43

but precisely the same as all the rest. We were not going to be able to adopt a baby.

When I came up against this barrage of identical answers, I was plunged into a mixture of feelings, not one of them good. Paramount in my mind was a sense of having been cheated by life. Again, I kept thinking why, why are things like this? I wanted a child so much, I felt we could give a baby just as good a home as anyone else. Yet at the same time I saw there were so few babies available for adoption that the authorities had to set some limits, and inevitably one of these would be age. Age tormented me now. I looked around at our peers, the people we knew of about our age. Nearly all of them had a child; it was almost as if it were wrong to have waited until I was thirty or so before considering a family. I felt 'if only I could have looked ahead, foreseen that this could happen . . .' But of course I couldn't have known, and besides, this line of thought was absurd, because we *had* tried – albeit accidentally – to start our family within six months of meeting each other, it was hardly as if we'd been putting it off and putting it off.

As with all arbitrary limits, there were things about the age restriction it was difficult to come to terms with. It particularly annoyed me at the time that we'd been offered a special needs child: I thought, well, we can have a child that has special needs, but we can't have a perfect baby, and that seemed to me very wrong, an odd sort of thinking seemed to be behind that kind of attitude.

Eventually I came to feel absolutely, totally hopeless. I felt I'd been batting my head against a brick wall. I didn't know what to do, or where to turn. There seemed to be no other avenues left open. I felt, that's it, there's nothing else to do; all my work, weeks and weeks of telephoning and writing to people, had led me to this – the knowledge that I couldn't have my own child and I couldn't adopt one.

But there was one other thing I couldn't do – accept this state of affairs. It was as if we'd been unjustly sentenced to a lifetime of barrenness, to a house empty of children's cries and laughter, to averting our eyes from prams and playgrounds, toyshops and swings: to a future that stopped with us. It was as if someone had said, 'I'm sorry, that's the end of your story, from now on you'll just have to go on skiing holidays, amuse yourselves somehow.' And I refused to accept that. Inside, I made up my mind, I said we'll find a way, no matter what, somehow we'll find a way.

I think that was when my mind returned to surrogacy. It seemed our only hope. I would have to find out more about it, if possible from people who had actually experienced it. In my ignorance, I thought there must be some public organization that dealt with such matters, so I went to our local library to see what I could unearth there. The librarian there was very helpful – God bless her soul. She said that apart from a few autobiographical books on the subject, as far as she knew there wasn't any source of information about surrogacy. But she remembered reading an article some years before about a woman in Scotland who'd either had, or received, a surrogate baby – she wasn't sure which. The librarian said she'd contact the local press for me to see if they could trace the article and give me this woman's name.

A few days later I got a phone call from the library. 'Mrs Walker? I've managed to trace that article for you. The name of the lady you're looking for is Mrs Gena Dodd, and I've also got a contact number for her . . .'

At last, I had it – a contact, a start. Someone positive to go to for help – hope – above all, hope. I wouldn't have to go on fumbling in the dark. Yet, like many moments where you have the chance to go forward from a state of ignorance into one of knowledge, now that I had this magic contact, in a way I was paralysed with fear: frightened of more disappointment, and of what it would mean if by some chance Mrs Dodd *could* help us, or knew of someone who could carry a child for us. For I hardly knew how I really felt about this as yet – I didn't know if or how I could cope with a third person being so intimately involved in such a private, precious part of our lives. I was also nervous about intruding on Mrs Dodd in this way, and, to make matters worse, I was confused about what had happened to her. I hardly knew who she was, whether she'd given birth to the baby, or had the baby by the surrogate. But, having come this far, I had to go on, I had to know at least whether there was any chance, however remote. I couldn't settle for being childless with the doubt niggling away forever in my mind that we might, after all, have been able to have a baby and just hadn't tried hard enough, hadn't explored every possible path. I had to know.

With this conviction in my mind, one day early in July I sat down in front of the telephone with Mrs Dodd's number on a notepad at my elbow. I looked at the number, then at the phone. Never had this harmless object seemed so terrifying. I got up and went into the kitchen to make myself some tea. I sat again, drinking the tea, and staring at the phone, almost willing it to ring so I could pretend I hadn't had a chance to call Mrs Dodd that day. I told myself not to be so daft. Then I thought, But what if she doesn't want to know, what if she slams the phone down on me? I'm a complete stranger, I can't just ring this woman up out of the blue!

I got up and returned to the kitchen for another cup of tea. I went back to the sitting room; the phone was still there, and the pad, with that number on it. I gulped my drink.

Alone in the silence I thought about everything that had happened in the past month, all the letters I'd written, the calls I'd made, and how it hadn't changed anything. I was still in the same boat, drifting hopelessly in the dark towards an empty horizon. It seemed to me I had a choice. I could stay where I was, childless in a sea of tears. Or I could call that number and, one last time, ask for help.

I shivered, and gripped my warm mug for comfort, and courage. Then I picked up the receiver and dialled Gena Dodd's number.

5

DISCOVERIES, DOUBTS
AND A DECISION

The voice on the end of the line sounded careful, but friendly enough. I said at once who I was and why I was ringing. To my huge relief, far from slamming the receiver down on me, Mrs Dodd – or Gena, as I quickly came to call her – answered me by explaining more about herself and what she did. As she spoke, my nervous grasp on my mug of tea gradually relaxed. At last I was communicating openly with someone about surrogacy: at last, here was a woman who knew from experience what I wanted to know.

Gena told me that about five years previously, having been childless for seventeen years for medical reasons, and after fruitlessly trying to adopt a child, she and her husband had asked or 'commissioned' a surrogate mother to have a baby for them, fathered by Mr Dodd. At the time, there were no laws regarding surrogacy, so Gena had been able to advertise quite openly for a surrogate and be completely honest about what she was doing. Since that time, however, the 1985 Surrogacy Arrangements Act had been passed, banning commercial surrogacy and making it illegal for anyone to advertise either for, or as, a prospective surrogate. This explained why it had been so difficult for me to track down any information about the subject.

Partly as a result of the flood of enquiries she received from people after her own story was reported in the press, and partly in response to the restrictions imposed by the Act, Gena had set up two organizations to help people interested in surrogacy. She was secretary of Childlessness Overcome Through Surrogacy (COTS), which gathered, collated and disseminated a wide range of information on all aspects of surrogacy. COTS was non-commercial, being entirely voluntary, since it was illegal for third parties to assist in

47

the practice of surrogacy for commercial gain. Gena had found, like me, that when she'd first looked into surrogacy there was almost no information on the subject, and she'd had to start more or less from scratch. She'd felt that because surrogacy was such a momentous, sensitive and complicated undertaking, there was a critical need for some kind of service to advise people responsibly about all the possible problems and pitfalls, as well as to attempt to pressurize the Government into recognizing that the existing legislation needed to be changed. This was what COTS tried to do.

Gena also ran a separate linkline service, Triangle, which put couples and prospective surrogate mothers in touch with each other. Again, the service was totally voluntary, and, as Gena put it, all she could do was to help people make contact – from then on, it was up to the individuals to arrange what they were going to do and how they were to go about it.

When I heard all this, my heart soared. Quite by chance, I seemed to have stumbled across a person who was the very nerve-centre of a whole surrogacy network I'd begun to despair of finding! However, all the way through this part of the conversation, I was still under the impression that what we were discussing was host surrogacy; it was only when I asked about the actual process of begetting a surrogate baby, and Gena started to explain some of the practicalities, that we found we were at slightly cross purposes.

Gena had mentioned that it was usual for a surrogate to inseminate herself using a syringe filled with the father's semen. I then asked, 'So how would we get my egg out, and into the surrogate mother?'

There was a flummoxed pause from the other end of the line while Gena wrestled with the implications of this question.

'Do you mean you would like a woman to be implanted with one of your eggs, already fertilized by your husband?'

'Yes – isn't that what *you* meant?'

'No, no – what you're talking about's a different matter, it's host surrogacy, and it's never yet been done in this country. You have to have a doctor to perform the egg retrieval, the IVF and the implantation. Because the Surrogacy Act is open to various interpretations where third party involvement is concerned, most doctors would never agree to get involved for fear of prosecution.'

'Oh, I see.'

The disappointment in my voice must have been palpable, for Gena said, 'You very much want your own baby then, do you, not one that has been conceived by somebody else?'

'Well, I'd been told medically this is possible. I know there are difficulties, but I was still hoping . . . What sort of surrogacy are you talking about then?'

Gena then explained that COTS was mainly concerned with what's simply called 'surrogacy' – where a woman conceives and bears her own biological child, using sperm from the 'commissioning' father, on the understanding that she gives up the baby to the commissioning couple at birth.

As I tried to think about the implications of this – for I'd never heard of this practice before – Gena must have sensed my hesitancy and dismay. She told me that if I really had set my heart on host surrogacy, I should be aware that she was in the process of writing to a number of doctors to find out whether they'd be prepared to assist in host arrangements, and that I should perhaps wait a while and see what sort of response she got. But she added that, to be perfectly honest, she didn't expect any positive outcome, and that we might do better to consider straightforward surrogacy instead – though she immediately warned me that surrogates were very few and far between, so it would help if I already knew of someone who would be prepared to be a surrogate, or we could be in for a long wait.

I asked a few more questions about surrogacy, such as what the legal position was, how one would arrange things with the surrogate, and so on. Gena said she could send me some more detailed information about it all, but made a few things clear there and then. She said that under the existing Surrogacy Act, there was nothing illegal about a private arrangement either to commission or give birth to a surrogate baby, providing no fee changed hands between third parties. The couple and the surrogate were considered to be 'outwith' the law – that is, they were allowed to do this – because the Government was anxious that any child born from such arrangements should not suffer from its parents being criminalized. However, she warned me that in law, the surrogate mother had absolute rights over the child, and, if she decided to keep it, there was virtually no chance of the couple ever getting custody. So, if we entered into surrogacy, we'd have to accept that there was no contract we could make to ensure the surrogate would give us the baby, and we'd have to live with the risk of her changing her mind and keeping it. This, Gena stressed, demanded a lot of strength on our part. Lastly, she said that though what we were considering was not illegal, it was still best to keep the matter as secret as possible. The reason for this was that, even if we were given the baby, there was a danger that the social services, which by and large took a dim view of surrogacy, would try to make the baby a ward-of-court. This would give the court the power to decide on the baby's future, and could mean the child was removed from our care. Though Gena said this was unlikely to happen once we had a chance to bond with the baby and it was living with us, the chief danger lay in news of the surrogacy leaking out before the birth. In that case the baby might well be made a ward-of-court in the hospital as soon as it was born – meaning we could lose it before we'd had any opportunity to care for it and so strengthen our case as its parents. It was therefore crucial to keep quiet about the whole thing for as long as possible, however difficult or unpleasant it might be to be driven as it were 'underground'.

When I'd heard her out, words failed me. It was too much to take in at once. But eventually I asked if she'd send me more details, and said I'd need some time to think things over. She said she'd put the information in the post and wait for my reply.

As I came off the phone my head was reeling and I felt slightly sick from the shock of what Gena had told me. She'd effectively advised that host surrogacy would be well-nigh impossible, and I thought to myself, 'That's it, a dream gone.'

Up until now, I'd still cherished the hope that someday we'd have our own genetic child, since I'd been told at the hospital that if we came back in about a year there might be a possibility of achieving this through host surrogacy if IVF facilities were installed. There's no doubt that at that time I felt, in theory at least, that this would have been far preferable to the form of surrogacy we'd now be considering. It was very hard for me to accept that another woman would give birth to a baby who wasn't my genetic child, although of course it would be Mark's. Apart from having to let this idea sink in, involving another person in the conception of the baby raised all sorts of questions about that person's medical history, which would somehow have to be answered before we could go ahead – that's always supposing Gena could find us a surrogate in the first place. On top of this, we'd have to be sure the woman would give up the baby – or as sure as anyone can be about such a highly emotional matter.

For me, particularly, it was all a very daunting prospect. I was only a few weeks out of a traumatic operation, and still struggling to come to terms with both my baby's death and the strangeness of losing my womb – something that had affected my image of myself as a woman. I knew I wouldn't be able to cope with another loss, should we embark on a surrogacy plan and the surrogate then decided to keep the baby. But what sort of amazing person could be trusted to give up her own child to someone else? It would have to be someone very, very special.

This was how both Mark and I thought of surrogate mothers, even then: neither of us had any moral reservations or qualms about surrogacy from that point of view. Other – usually fertile – people might casually condemn a woman for giving up 'her' baby, but for us it seemed the surrogates Gena had told us about must be very remarkable women, capable of undergoing a good deal of inconvenience, physical discomfort, effort and pain in order, essentially, to give a childless couple the ultimate gift of a longed-for baby. I knew in my own mind that the only person *I* could ever have acted as a surrogate for was my sister: I couldn't have given up 'my' baby to people who were strangers. And, as a matter of fact, when I'd first been wondering about host surrogacy, my sister Megan had said that she'd be prepared to act as the host mother for us if we could find a doctor who was prepared to do the IVF and implantation. However, her then fiancé (now her husband), Eamon, was deeply opposed to the idea; and when I discussed the other kind of surrogacy with Megan, she felt she couldn't do it, not if the baby was genetically hers. In any case, my mother had told me she felt it would be very unwise to involve a relative in *this* kind of surrogacy. She pointed out, very sensibly, that although Megan and I are very close, as in any sibling relationship there are things about each other we find irritating. How would I cope if the baby inherited some of these traits from Megan? Or what if we had a family row one day, and all these things were dragged up? And wouldn't I find it difficult to feel really secure as the baby's mother if my sister had conceived the baby and was living, as she did, close by, always there, as it were looking over my shoulder? Mum was right – these were very important considerations. Yet where on earth were we going to find a stranger to be our surrogate; someone who when the time came would have the strength of mind to hand us the baby, who would surely do that?

But if it seemed unlikely we'd ever find a suitable surrogate, we were hardly in a position in which we could opt not to pursue this avenue, however fraught the way ahead seemed. For host surrogacy could scarcely be considered, now, to be a realistic option, however desirable it might be. Apart from Gena's comments about the legal problems, we also knew from the hospital that there was only about a twenty percent success rate in achieving implantation of the fertilized egg. Secondly, the cost of each attempt was around £2,000 – with no guarantee of success. I knew that if the odds had been better, we'd have been prepared to spend such sums, and even sell the flat if we had to, in order to conceive our own child. But with such a low success rate, we had to face the possibility that we might spend as much as £12,000 and still be childless. And what sort of state would I be in, emotionally, if after six attempts we were no nearer to having a baby, and impoverished into the bargain, so that we wouldn't be able to try any other avenues?

As the days passed, we knew we didn't really have a choice: it was surrogacy or nothing. So, about a week after I'd first spoken to Gena, I took a deep breath, called her back to say that we were still interested in surrogacy and, should she hear of a potential surrogate, could she please get in touch with us. We sent her some basic details about ourselves, so she could circulate them to anyone considering becoming a surrogate. Then there seemed to be nothing left to do but settle down for a long wait.

In the meantime, true to her word, Gena sent me down a whole library's worth of material on surrogacy, and during July I plundered it for everything I could find. So, in a welter of information and a snowstorm of paperwork, the month passed by. Though to all intents and purposes, I must have appeared extremely busy and well on the road to recovery, in fact my life seemed to be stuck in a rut like an old cart; frankly, I felt I was going nowhere. Though my body had healed, there were the other, deeper wounds to my heart and soul, and no matter what I did, these were still as raw as when they'd first been inflicted. I was in an emotional abyss until Emma's cremation. Yet thinking of the day itself, with all its approaching sorrow, hardly brought peace of mind. I was filled with a tension comprised of longing and dread.

I shall remember 29 July 1988 for as long as I live. We had ordered a little posy of roses to take with us to lay on top of the coffin, and while Mark went to collect the flowers, I tried to get dressed and ready, all the while shaking like a leaf. Mark returned, and gave me the card to write our goodbye. It read: 'Emma, how much we loved you darling, you're with us today and will remain in our hearts, in our thoughts, in our memories, forever, farewell my darling, Mum and Dad xxx.' Mark placed the card in the posy, then hugged me tightly and said it was time to go. Inside, I felt a lump in my throat and a terrible emptiness. I needed to cry so badly, but I wanted to arrive at the service composed. I took one look at Mark and knew he was feeling exactly the same, but was trying so hard to be strong for me.

As we approached the west chapel of the crematorium my tears began; I was choking inside. I kissed the posy before it was taken away to be placed on the coffin. Slowly, we walked into the chapel and sat down. Rev. Swinton began the service by saying it was one of cremation for all pregnancies which fail to go to term, that these were small human beings whom we wished to acknowledge and remember always. He spoke of the hospital staff who had tried so hard to help, but couldn't in the end; of all those people doing research to try and prevent these tragedies; and of those near to us who were feeling for and thinking of us all today. Then there were prayers. We said the Lord's Prayer, and the Reverend spoke some other words of devotion; and there followed a moment of silent prayer. Then he said, 'We now commit these pregnancies that have failed to reach maturity to be cremated. Ashes to ashes: dust to dust.'

My heart broke as I saw the curtains close around the tiny coffin.

That was our last farewell. Though it was harrowing, the service also brought great comfort. Rev. Swinton's words were very moving and gave Emma and the other babies great dignity. It was a tremendous relief to us to know that she had actually been properly laid to rest, and I'll always be very grateful to the Reverend for offering us the service and for all the support he has given us since then. As far as we know, his service in Aberdeen is unique in the United Kingdom; surely it would be a good thing for more ministers to offer this kind of vital comfort and recognition to the parents and babies who suffer as we did.

After the service, I felt more at peace. But hardly had I recovered from the tension leading up to that day when I received news that was to plunge us into a different sort of turmoil. One morning towards the end of July, Gena rang. It was quite early, and I was still lying in bed, with all my thousands of papers about adoption and so on strewn around me. As I reached for the receiver there was nothing to suggest I was about to answer the most devastating phone call of my life.

Gena sounded as calm as ever. She asked me whether we were still ready to go ahead with surrogacy, and I said yes, we were very keen. But nothing gave me an inkling as to what was coming next.

'Okay, Rona. Well, I think I possibly have a woman who's prepared to be a surrogate for you.'

I couldn't believe my ears! It was certainly no more than four or five weeks since I'd first spoken to Gena – since, indeed, she'd explained to me that surrogates were few and far between and that we'd have to be prepared to wait for months, maybe even years, before she found someone. And now here she was telling me there was a woman ready and waiting for us! I froze.

Gena continued, 'She's here with me now, actually.'

And then my panic set in, most unexpectedly, but with great force. We'd wanted this moment so badly; yet here we were, faced with a real opportunity, and I didn't know what to do. I have to say I felt like changing my mind there and then, I was so bewildered.

Gena, unaware of the cataclysmic effect of her words so far, went on steadily. 'Would you like to speak to her?'

This time my reaction was immediate. 'No, no, we have to come and speak to you first, before we come anywhere near anyone else, we have to speak to you . . .'

There was a pause. My mind reeling, I tried to sound more positive.

'Look Gena. I need a moment to take this in. Let me speak to Mark, then I'll call you back tomorrow, maybe I could speak to her then . . .'

She agreed, and rang off. And I beat a hasty retreat to the kitchen, to make myself another cup of tea.

It was like a dream, but somehow, surprisingly, not a happy dream. In fact I felt more as if I'd prepared carefully for an exam, only to find on reading the first question that all my knowledge had flown straight out of my head and I knew nothing. I'd thought we'd decided, yes, we were going ahead with surrogacy, I thought I'd made up my mind and come to terms with it; this was our only chance. But it seemed that now we really had that chance, far from jumping at it, we weren't sure we were going to take it at all. I suppose the point was that it had seemed so unlikely we'd actually find a surrogate that all our considerations had been simply theoretical, rather than real, concrete decisions. To an outsider, it may seem strange that I felt in such a panic: surely, you might say, we could go and meet the woman anyway, and *then* decide? Realistically speaking, this was true, and certainly, even in the heat of the moment, Mark felt we could meet her and still walk away from the situation if need be. But I felt differently. I'd been completely engrossed in somehow having another baby ever since I'd woken in hospital and been told what had happened. Having a child had become my life, my purpose. Now here was a chance. I knew surrogates didn't grow on trees, that if we didn't 'commission' a baby now we might be faced with years of childlessness. In the barren weeks I'd already lived through since 28 May I had begun to understand just what that might mean, what it might do to me, and I was afraid of that knowledge.

And yet . . . And yet, I was also frightened at the prospect that lay ahead. I felt very strongly that we weren't ready; surely, we'd hardly adjusted to the notion of surrogacy, we didn't really know what it would mean. I particularly was still coming to terms with the fact that the surrogate would be so closely involved with creating the baby; now that I knew there was a woman there, waiting, I wondered if it might not be best if I never met her, even if we went ahead. Surely, Mark could just provide the semen samples, there was no need for *me* to meet the surrogate. Essentially, I was petrified of suffering another loss. If we went into this and, horror of horrors, the surrogate decided to keep the baby, I felt that if we'd never met, then I could still keep my distance – she'd always be a stranger to me, and I might (or so I rather confusedly reasoned) remain detached from the whole business. Mark, however, pointed out that this was a bit absurd, and added that I'd have to meet her for my own peace of mind, or I'd always be wondering what she was like. In any case, he said, he wasn't going to be left to face the music on his own!

So, eventually, I rang Gena back to see if we should arrange a meeting. I said that possibly, it might be a good idea for us to see Stephanie Cottam, the prospective surrogate, as well – I wasn't sure. In fact, Stephanie was staying with Gena at that point, so this time, when Gena offered me the chance to speak to her, I agreed. Incredibly, I found myself waiting to talk to a complete stranger who might become the woman who'd bear us a child. It was a momentous event.

My heart pounded as I listened for the voice on the other end of the line. There was a long, long, expectant silence. I couldn't tell if Stephanie was there or not; whether I was meant to speak first, or wait for her to, or what. My throat was parched and thirsting, as if I'd swallowed a desert and was choking on sand. I felt I'd never be able to utter a word. The silence hummed on.

At last I could bear it no longer.

I took a deep breath. 'Hello Stephanie, how are you?'

'Yes, hello, fine thanks. And you?'

Well, what *could* I say? The whole subject seemed so enormous, it's no wonder the talk started off rather small. Gradually I got down to something more like brass tacks. I asked how long she'd thought about it all, because I said *we'd* been thinking of nothing else for weeks, and we wanted to be sure she wasn't just rushing into it, that she'd thought it through . . . There was an irony here, as it turned out that while we'd known about surrogacy for all of five weeks, Stephanie had been considering becoming a surrogate for three years! In that time, as we were to discover, she'd certainly thought about everything very, very thoroughly; it was hardly a spur of the moment decision. As we chatted, I saw there were so many things we needed to ask and discuss, it did seem better that we should all meet. Stephanie was very keen to arrange this as soon as possible. So somehow I found myself arranging for us to drive over to Gena's in about a week's time.

For the rest of that day I just panicked all over again. I

was excited, but petrified at what we seemed to be getting into: above all, I think the speed at which everything seemed to be happening really worried me, being by nature rather cautious. And now I'd spoken to Stephanie, it all seemed that much more real. What had been a faint possibility was fast becoming a reality. How would we cope?

The irony was that all along, since May, everyone I'd spoken to had told me to take things easy, give myself time, not to rush. And of course, at that point, I'd spurned such advice. I'd had to be *doing*, planning, taking steps to improve things, to make things happen. Only now, as I sat facing the consequence of my frenzied activity, did I feel pressurized, as if everything was indeed going too fast, and perhaps I should climb out of this rollercoaster before some unguessable and irrevocable future hurtled towards me.

In the end, I got myself so confused, I decided to ring Kim Cotton, who was chairperson of COTS and who had herself been a surrogate mother. As soon as I told her how I felt, she said at once that I should just forget about going ahead. It was a major decision, she said; we needed to think long and hard before we got anywhere near going to meet Stephanie. She made me see that none of this was inevitable. We did have a choice!

This alone made me feel a lot better; then, a few minutes later, Gena rang. She told me she'd just had Kim on the phone telling her off for upsetting me, and said that hadn't been her intention at all, she was very sorry if I felt pressurized. By now, I was so much calmer, it didn't take long for us to sort things out. I must point out that Gena was only doing what she thought best – telling us the good news! It was simply my panic which had thrown me into confusion. We agreed to go ahead with the meeting as arranged, but on the clear understanding that neither we nor Stephanie should feel we had to proceed.

As I rang off, I felt reassured. After all, Gena had every reason to expect us to be keen to meet Stephanie; we'd urged her to contact us as soon as she found a surrogate. And, in the normal run of things, the other couples she'd helped had been pretty keen to get matters under way as soon as possible, since very often they'd had a long history of infertility and Gena's call was the light at the end of a very long, black, childless tunnel. In any case we now had a week to get our feelings and ideas sorted out before meeting Stephanie.

In that week we talked of nothing else. We started to understand what a huge step we were taking. Gena had told us to get everything clear from the outset, and there seemed so many aspects to consider: legal, financial, medical, practical, emotional. Definitely, surrogacy is not for the faint- or half-hearted. We had to look so far ahead: before even deciding to try for a baby, we had to think about what sort of arrangement we'd have with Stephanie after the birth, when she'd given us the child – would we break all ties, or still keep in touch? It was horrendous trying to think of every eventuality. And even when we'd written down a list of questions as long as your arm, there were still some we knew only time could answer, such as would we like Stephanie?

It really was a heart-searching process. We had to be very hard-headed, rational and clear about something which touched us both deeply emotionally, but which we knew little about. One of the hardest things was not being able to talk about it openly with everyone. We just had to make the rules up as we went along and decide, alone, what to do. At times it felt as if we were totally in the dark, totally on our own. This was a huge burden, and made it difficult to prepare for meeting Gena and Stephanie, because we didn't know whether we'd thought of all the questions we should be asking. Talking about it to my mother and sister helped; but of course neither of them had ever done anything like this before either . . .

In the end we confided in our friend Susan, who worked at an infertility clinic. She proved to be an absolute mine of helpful advice, information – and first-hand experience. For lo and behold, when I mentioned that we were considering surrogacy, she revealed that in the course of her midwifery career she'd actually delivered a surrogate baby! So she not only brought up topics we hadn't thought about – such as what we would do if a scan showed the baby was handicapped or deformed – but she also made me understand fully what *my* position would be in all this. Though I hadn't been aware of it, all through our chat I'd obviously been referring to the potential child as 'Stephanie's baby'. Susan told me in no uncertain terms that I must get it into my head that it would be mine and Mark's, not Stephanie's. She told me not to defer to Stephanie about it: her view was that if Stephanie became a surrogate for us, she'd be doing a wonderful thing, but it was essentially a job; a job she had decided to do of her own free will. We must think of the baby as ours, and feel we had the right to decide on many matters concerning its health and so on, just as if I were pregnant with the child myself. In practice I don't think the situation ever seems as clear-cut as this – we were always aware that it was Stephanie's life, and her body too, we were involved with – but it was very helpful to us to have Susan spell things out like this. It gave me more confidence to recognize that I would be the baby's mother, and must have my say.

Lastly, Susan urged us to consult a solicitor. Even if we couldn't draw up a watertight contract that would be enforceable in the courts, we should still have legal advice. That way we would at least have an informed mind behind us to fall back on should we run into problems, and someone detached from the situation to turn to at moments when we were in an emotional turmoil.

Susan's advice was invaluable. It was as if she'd lifted a ton off our shoulders, and brought us down to earth. As we left her we felt that at last, we'd begun to understand the reality of surrogacy and all its implications.

For the rest of that week, we double- and triple-checked our list of questions, and counted the minutes off to 'D-Day'. Sure enough, eventually it came, and we set off for Gena's. Though we must have driven through some breathtaking scenery on the way, neither of us noticed a thing outside: we just talked and talked about the forthcoming event. I was as nervous as I'd ever been; Mark was a bit more detached, and, truth to tell, quite suspicious. He thought it odd that we'd originally been warned it could take years to find a surrogate, and now, just five or six weeks later, here we were going to meet one. I think for Mark it was as much a fact-finding mission as anything else, though he'd agreed that, if all went well, we should suggest to Stephanie that we should start getting to know each other first, before preparing to try for a baby.

'Try for a baby.' That incredible prospect underlay everything I felt as we arrived at Gena's that day. Despite all my fears and reservations, my doubts and dilemmas, as we reached the front door and rang the bell, my hopes were high and my heart was in my mouth.

6
SURROGACY . . . AND STEPHANIE

Gena showed us into the sitting room, where we met her husband, Michael, and five-year-old John, their son – living proof that surrogacy was a real possibility. He looked at me, and I looked at him, and wondered if Mark and I, too, might one day have just such a miracle living with us.

For the moment, however, all we had were hopes, fears, and that great long list of questions. Gena told us that Stephanie was here, but had agreed to wait in another part of the house while we had a preliminary chat with Gena about surrogacy; and she set about answering our queries. As she spoke, our doubts and worries about who she was and whether COTS really was bona fide all fell away. She was obviously a most genuine, straightforward and compassionate person, committed to helping childless couples and surrogates as far as she possibly could. And she knew what she was talking about.

First, she ran through the legal position. As she'd already told us, commissioning and bearing surrogate babies were not in themselves illegal activities: but paying someone, or being paid, to act on behalf of either party in order to get a child, was. This was why Gena worked entirely voluntarily. It was also one reason why doctors and lawyers were often very wary of involvement in surrogacy, and this and the ambiguities in the existing Surrogacy Act had resulted in the conspiracy of silence which now surrounded the subject and made it all seem like a criminal activity.

She reiterated that in law, the surrogate mother had total rights over the baby. Should she decide to keep it, we had almost no chance of getting custody. We could try, by applying for a ward-of-courtship on the child and fighting the case in court as soon as possible, before the mother had

had an opportunity to bond with the baby: but our chances of success would be extremely slim. And there was no legal measure that could be taken prior to the birth to ensure the baby would be given to us. Essentially, we'd be relying on sheer naked trust. That was risk number one.

'Now,' said Gena, 'if the surrogate does give you the baby, the next risk is how the court reacts when you apply to adopt the child.'

Mark and I both froze. Then, before we could think, we both blurted out, '*What? Adopt* the baby?'

Mark added incredulously, 'Why do I have to adopt my own child?'

Gena, seeing the absolute shock, even horror, on our faces, agreed. 'Yes, I know it sounds awful, and it *is* awful. But in law, because the baby will be born out of wedlock, because it won't be living with its biological mother, and because its biological parents won't be living together, you're both going to have to apply as a couple to adopt the child. I know, Mark, it's your genetic child, but I'm afraid that's the only way you and Rona are going to secure your legal rights as parents, and have your baby safely in your care once and for all. Otherwise, if Stephanie gives you the child, you'd still have to fight for custody in court if she ever changed her mind.'

She stopped, letting this sink in. She must have registered from our reaction that it was a bitter blow. It opened up a whole new set of problems; to have to deal with adoption as well as worrying about the surrogacy arrangements was bewildering. After a very pregnant pause, in which both of us could hardly refrain from raining down curses on the Government and its laws, I finally asked, 'Can you tell us what adoption would involve?'

'Yes. You remember I told you on the phone about the need for secrecy?'

I nodded. 'You said something about wards-of-court, but I'm afraid I didn't really take in what that was about.'

'Well, this is all connected to the adoption. It's best to keep quiet about the fact you're having a surrogate baby, at least until the baby's born and in your home. This is to try to ensure the social services don't find out before you've had a chance to bond with the baby. I know that sounds bad, but the fact is, until you've adopted the child, you won't have legal rights over it, and if the social services discover you're about to have a surrogate baby, or find out just after it's born, they might try to make it a ward-of-court before you've established any relationship with it.'

'What would happen then?' I asked.

'The court would have the right to decide who should look after the baby; and you wouldn't have any rights to the child, because you wouldn't legally be recognized as its parents.'

Seeing we were about to exclaim in outraged dismay, Gena went on quickly, 'Now, if you take the child home as soon as possible after the birth, without anyone finding out it's a surrogate baby, you have a chance to bond with it. When the social services eventually find out – which they will, because sooner or later you'll have to apply to adopt – they might still make the child a ward-of-court, until the adoption's approved. But even if they do that, it's very unlikely the baby would be taken away from you. Normally the court would have no grounds for doing this unless you were ill-treating or neglecting the baby. The authorities are going to have to take into account that the surrogate mother's prepared to give you the baby; that Mark, you're its natural father, and Rona, you're his wife; that you're willing as a couple to bring it up as your own; and that you're going to be applying to adopt the child at some point. All that should weigh very heavily in your favour. And if it's any consolation, I know of no case in which, when a surrogate has given up the baby, the couple haven't subsequently been granted adoption.'

We perked up slightly at this news. Mark asked, 'Is there anything else we should know about this?'

'Yes. It's illegal to pay or receive money for a child – the Government rightly outlaws this to prevent a trade in babies. So from your point of view, though there's nothing in black-and-white in the Surrogacy Act about paying the surrogate, if you did actually pay her a fee, that could endanger your application to adopt the baby. So you need to be careful there. The other thing you should know is that under Scottish law, adoption can't be granted until the baby's at least five months old, and in practice, it's not usually granted before the child's first birthday. So you'll have a long period of waiting, which is always an ordeal. From the moment the baby's born, you'll experience all this anxiety as parents of a child you desperately want, so it will be especially hard to accept that for a while you'll have no legal rights over its future. You'll have to be very strong.'

We glanced at each other. After a brief pause, Mark smiled at me and said, 'I think we can manage that. Rona?'

I grinned. 'Oh yes. On a good day . . .' Then I turned to Gena. 'Are there any other problems with social services?'

'The main thing is keeping the surrogacy secret for as long as you can. By law, all newborn babies and their mothers have to be visited by a midwife for the first ten days after the birth, and thereafter they're assigned to a health visitor. So at some point you're going to have to inform the social services of your situation to make sure the baby and the surrogate receive proper medical care. Now, if you take the baby home as soon as it's discharged from hospital, and the surrogate goes to another home, obviously the social services might guess at once it's a surrogate baby, since the mother and child won't be living together. As I say, that doesn't have to be a disaster; you'll already have the baby in your home. But you can delay the social services finding out, without putting anyone's health at risk, if you arrange for all of you to stay together in one place until those crucial ten days have elapsed. Then you don't have to say it's a surrogate baby, though once the surrogate's left you, you'll have to tell the health visitor who subsequently sees the baby that you're adopting.'

'Right.' It all seemed horrendously complicated, and I hated the feeling that we would have to lie, as if somehow we were criminals involved in some sinister cloak-and-dagger plot. We were trying to have a baby, not harm anyone or break the law.

I felt if it was going to be as hard as this, we had to know what our chances of actually being given the baby were. 'Have you ever known of a surrogate who wouldn't give the couple the child?'

Gena said, 'Yes, that has happened – but I've only ever

heard of one such case. There's no way of guaranteeing any woman will give up a baby – people change during pregnancy, and childbirth is a very emotional experience. But you can help the surrogate not to grow too attached to the baby if you give her a lot of support during the pregnancy and labour, and I normally advise surrogates not to breastfeed after the birth, but to give the baby to the couple as soon as possible. I know that may seem hard on the surrogate, but it's to save her unnecessary pain and grief – and stop her having second thoughts. If she does this, the baby doesn't have to be deprived of breastmilk – *you* could breastfeed if you wanted to.'

I was flabbergasted – but this time with delight. 'I've always wanted to breastfeed my baby! I didn't know you could do that!'

'Oh yes. It is possible, if the child is very young. I can give you more details later . . .'

I didn't hesitate. 'Yes please!'

All of a sudden, things seemed to be looking up. Perhaps surrogacy wasn't going to be all stress and strain after all – there might be room for a few bright, joyful moments too; some simple, essential pleasures, such as suckling a newborn baby.

Fuelled with fresh hope, we consulted our list of questions for the next item on the agenda. It was a tricky one: finance. Gena said that she could only give us guidelines; the particular agreement we made with Stephanie, if we made one, was entirely our business. There were no charges for Gena's own role as linkline and adviser. She reiterated that the law on this aspect of surrogacy – as on many others – was a mess: there was nothing specifically banning payment of a surrogate, but she felt that paying a fee might jeopardize the adoption. However, she suggested that paying the surrogate's expenses might be acceptable. These might include any time the surrogate had to take off work because of the pregnancy and birth; any medical care she might need; child care if she had any other children already; maternity clothes; extra food or dietary needs; and insurance. Gena explained that before they entered into any arrangement, she always clearly advised potential surrogates of the risk that they might die in childbirth. Then, the surrogate often took out an insurance policy for herself for twelve months, and the couple paid the premiums. On top of these expenses, some couples paid for accommodation and travel costs if the surrogate moved to be near them; and of course there would be solicitors' fees to pay if we took legal advice on the matter. Last, but not least, there was the equipment needed for the actual insemination. Gena herself could provide, free of charge, a special syringe with which the surrogate could inseminate herself, but it was also useful to buy ovulation kits, and a digital thermometer, which would help to show when the surrogate was actually ovulating, or fertile. We might also wish to buy pregnancy testing kits.

Mark and I paused a moment here, trying to do some furious mental arithmetic. Clearly, surrogacy would be an undertaking, but it could have been a lot, lot worse. It looked at least as if we would still have the flat, and Mark's shirt could stay on his back – for the time being anyway.

We now had to find out about the medical side of things. This was a very important issue for us: was there any way of making sure that the surrogate was healthy, that there were no genetic disorders or hereditary diseases in her family? Mark and I both knew that we wouldn't wish to go ahead if there was a likelihood that the surrogate might bear a severely handicapped child; and, though we'd agonized over making the decision, we knew we would wish the pregnancy to be terminated if a scan showed the baby was badly deformed or handicapped. This had nothing to do with it being a surrogate baby. We'd have done the same had the baby been conceived in my body in the normal way.

Gena said there was no way we could gain access to the surrogate's medical records – these were strictly confidential. We could ask her to go to her GP for a medical – and take it on trust that she had done so – or we could pay for her to have one privately. But as far as her family history was concerned, this had to be taken on trust; there was simply no way of knowing, once and for all, other than by asking the surrogate and taking her word for it. This, Gena said, might seem dismaying, but she pointed out that the surrogate, too, had to take many things on trust. She had to trust that Mark was healthy, and not carrying any disease that could be transmitted via his semen – a particularly sensitive issue now, in the age of AIDS. Gena thought it was always sensible to request a surrogate to have an AIDS test, but that in that case, the surrogate had every right to ask the couple to undergo the test as well. As far as any health problems during the pregnancy were concerned, she told us that, obviously, even with scans and blood tests, there was no provision that could be made to guarantee a healthy, perfect baby, but that it would be up to us to discuss with Stephanie in advance what we would wish to happen in the event of an abnormality being discovered, and also to state whether we wanted her to undergo particular tests during pregnancy.

The medical uncertainties seemed huge when considered like this, all together. Mark and I felt daunted and frustrated, and I said, 'Why doesn't the Government get its act together! It's crazy that the law is such a mess. If they licensed surrogacy, it could be dealt with properly, openly, under medical supervision; all these risks could be minimized. My God, so many things in pregnancy and childbirth can go wrong –' I was speaking from bitter, first-hand experience ' – They're just making the whole thing even more dangerous.'

Mark agreed, but added, 'If we're going to take this opportunity, we've got to be positive and tell ourselves that many of the risks would be there even if we were conceiving in the normal way.'

'If it's any help,' Gena said, 'you're not alone in having to take so much on trust. The surrogate's going to have to trust you, too. She's going to trust that you'll support her when she's pregnant; that you'll see it through and accept the baby at the end – I know, it's hard for you to imagine refusing; but *she* doesn't know you yet! She'll also have to trust that you'll always love and care for the baby. So it's just as hard for her.'

This hit home. I said, 'Yes, I suppose if we go ahead, we're all going to have to accept there are things we can't control.' Simply saying it made me see how difficult that would be.

Mark must have seen the doubts gathering like clouds in my eyes, for he said, 'But if we all work together, in good faith, we may have a child.'

I smiled. There was only one answer to that. 'Aye, you're right enough.'

Gena, seeing me looking brighter once more, asked if she should now explain the practicalities involved in conceiving a surrogate baby. I think our heads were reeling, just slightly, by this time, but we both had no hesitation in saying yes. We might be a bit daunted, but we weren't defeated. To our relief, the mechanics of it all seemed relatively simple. Gena said that it had been known for the couple and surrogate to conceive in the natural way, but by and large, most people avoided this and opted for artificial self-insemination. We already knew that this was the method we wanted to use: I would never have considered any other. Gena said it involved the surrogate monitoring herself very carefully so that she became familiar with the pattern of her menstrual cycle, and knew when she was ovulating and ready to conceive. This was critical, as there are only a very few days in a woman's cycle when conception is likely to occur. It was useful for the surrogate to check her temperature at the same time each day – there is a change in the woman's body temperature when she is ovulating – using a digital thermometer. This was best done first thing in the morning, before the surrogate got out of bed and had any form of drink or food. Then, towards the middle of her cycle, she could use the ovulation kit to determine if she was ovulating. When she was, the commissioning father had to ejaculate into a small sterile container, wait ten minutes for the semen to become less viscous, and give this to the surrogate. She inseminated herself by drawing up the semen into a sterile ten ml syringe (without a needle of course!), which she then inserted into her vagina, expressing the semen from the syringe while lying down. It was best for her to stay supine for several hours, to prevent the semen from flowing out of her body, and to give the sperm a chance to swim up into the uterus; so insemination was usually done at night, just before the surrogate went to sleep.

There were a few other guidelines to follow. Obviously, the surrogate had to abstain from intercourse with anyone else when she was ovulating, and if she had intercourse at any other time in her cycle, she must use one of the barrier forms of birth control – the cap or the sheath. For his part, the commissioning husband should abstain from intercourse for about four or five days before the surrogate was due to ovulate, as well as for the days when she was ovulating, so that he built up a high sperm count and increased the chances of conceiving. So, although the process was fairly straightforward, it would involve restrictions on all of our sex lives which we would have to accept from the start. And, as a postscript, Gena added that we should not expect success first time. It could take at least six months, if not longer.

Apart from this, there were a few more tips she could give us about arranging matters with the surrogate. Again, she urged us to settle every detail at the outset, so we all knew exactly where we stood. She advised us to let the surrogate see us in our home, so she would know the kind of environment in which the child would grow up – something which might help our case when it came to informing the social services. Then there were four letters she suggested we write: one by Mark, stating that he was the biological father, and promised to love and care for the child; one addressed to us from the surrogate, stating that she promised to give us the child; one written by her, willing the baby to go to its natural father (Mark) in the event of her death in childbirth (normally, in cases where this happens and the father is unknown, the baby is put up for adoption); and fourthly, a letter from the surrogate stating that she gives the baby up willingly to its father and his wife, knowing it will have a loving, stable and happy home. This could be shown to the visiting midwife in the first few days after the birth, if the surrogate didn't stay in the same place as the baby for this period, so there'd be no suspicion that the couple had snatched the baby. These letters weren't legally enforceable, but might help our peace of mind and could be useful in dealing with the social services.

Gena reminded us that, however regrettable and unpleasant, it was best to keep the whole matter as secret as possible until we had the baby in our care, and preferably until we applied to adopt. She also told us, however, that we would need someone we could confide in, to help us carry the burden of all the anxiety, excitement and waiting. Once the baby was born, it should have as little contact as possible with the surrogate, to prevent bonding and distress – it would be nurtured by, and bond with, us instead – and we must register it as soon as we could, in Mark's and the surrogate's names. We should then apply for adoption once the child had been in our home for a reasonable time. Lastly, she said that if we had any skeletons in our cupboard, we should think very carefully about going ahead; it would be heartbreaking to conceive and have a surrogate baby, only to be denied adoption rights because of something in our family or personal history.

'Now,' Gena said, 'shall I tell you a bit about Stephanie?'

I swallowed hard, glanced at Mark, and nodded. As a lead-in, Gena told us something about the role of the surrogate, because she felt it was important for couples to see things from that point of view and adjust to the woman's needs if they were all to be able to work successfully together. She said that COTS concentrated on giving a lot of support to surrogates, emotionally: as she put it, 'As a couple, you've got a definite goal to aim for in all this: you will eventually have a baby. But the surrogate has to go through a lot on your behalf: nine months of pregnancy, in which she usually has to pretend the child is hers, and so lives a lie; going into hospital; the birth; staying in hospital with the newborn baby, but not being able to treat it as her own; coming out of hospital and giving up the baby; and then going home again with nothing.'

She went on to say that for these reasons, surrogates were usually married women, who already had children of their own, and therefore had both support from a family and experience of childbearing. In themselves, these were not

71

factors that could guarantee the surrogate would give up the child – nothing could ensure that – and no one could tell in advance how a surrogate would respond to a particular pregnancy, or a particular baby.

Stephanie was unusual for a surrogate in that she was not only unmarried and childless, but also very young – nineteen years old. Normally, Gena said she was very wary of agreeing to put forward such young women as prospective surrogates, but in this case, she had vetted Stephanie extremely carefully over a long period of time, and was satisfied that she knew what she was doing, she was going into it with her eyes wide open, and was determined to see it through. What had happened was this. Stephanie was a distant relative of Gena's, and had become interested in surrogacy through knowing of Gena's experience. When Stephanie was only sixteen, she'd come to Gena to say she was interested in becoming a surrogate and wanted more information. Gena had immediately sent her away, telling her not to be silly, she was far too young and didn't know what she was talking about. But twelve months later, she'd come back to Gena, still very keen after apparently having considered the matter very carefully. Gena had then given her a lot of leaflets about surrogacy, and told her to read them, plus Kim Cotton's account of her own experience of being a surrogate; and to contact several other surrogates and discuss their experiences. Then Stephanie should consider the whole thing again, especially the fact that she would have to live a lie for months, and could not know how she'd react to having her first child and giving it up forever. Gena had added firmly that she didn't want to hear from Stephanie about this for at least another year.

Sure enough, a year later, Stephanie was back again, undeterred, better informed and keener than ever. Gena had then taken her through the whole process step by step, and in the end, felt she was as satisfied as she ever had been or could be that Stephanie would be suitable, was fully aware of all the potential difficulties, and, most importantly, would give up the baby. Gena said we must judge for ourselves, but added that there was an advantage from our point of view in that there were some physical similarities between myself and Stephanie. Obviously, these were only superficial – we were about the same height and of more or less the same build, with similar colouring – but it would mean there was at least some physical compatibility.

'But anyway,' Gena finished, 'I think it's best if you see her yourselves. She's upstairs, so I'll just go and get her.'

And off she went.

Mark and I grimaced at each other with nerves. We were both full of trepidation. Meeting Stephanie might be the last hurdle, and now that we knew so much more about surrogacy, the suspense of waiting even a minute longer was unbearable. We heard Gena open a door upstairs; a pause; a muffled exchange; and then footsteps on the stairs. Moments later the sitting-room door was opened and in came Stephanie.

She sat down, looking remarkably calm and unflustered – and pretty much as Gena had described, excepting that she also had a fine, porcelain-white complexion and beautiful blue eyes. There was a lively quality about her, something very chirpy and happy-go-lucky, but at the same time, as we quickly discovered, she had none of the flightiness those words might suggest. Instead, as soon as she started talking, we found that in many ways she was far more mature and apparently confident than most people of her age. She had very set ideas, and very *sensible* ideas, about the surrogacy situation, and she was clearly very well informed. Above all, the more we talked, the more obvious it was that she had thought all this out for herself, and was very, very determined.

Some of this determination came through as she answered our questions about her family background and how her parents felt about what she was doing. Her mother had been very supportive, saying she was happy as long as Stephanie was. She intended to come up and visit her at some point as well; it was clear they were very close. Her father, too, had been reasonably happy about it: however, there had been some problems with her stepfather, who was pretty opposed to the whole idea. The way Stephanie spoke about this showed she thought carefully about people's reactions, instead of just dismissing them. She said she felt he was really opposed to it because he was worried for her – worried that something might go wrong, and that she might not be able to cope afterwards. Although she said it was a shame he didn't approve, at least it was nice to know he was so concerned; and certainly she seemed undeterred by his reaction. Her independence was also plain to see from the fact she'd been prepared to give up her job and leave her home town to come and live at Gena's while she waited to move near whoever she was to act as a surrogate for.

Having heard a bit about herself and her family, we next had to ask the really burning question, which was why she wanted to be a surrogate. We both felt that a lot depended on how she responded to this: it would give us clues as to how far she'd thought about the possible problems, what her attitude towards having children was, and so on – in short, was she really aware of what she was doing. That may sound terribly suspicious and patronizing, but at this stage we didn't know Stephanie at all; all we knew was that she was very young, and had never had a baby, and might be getting into something she'd bitterly regret forever after. And none of us could afford to take unnecessary chances on that.

But it wasn't easy getting down to the nitty-gritty. There seemed to be no way of slipping the question in casually: it loomed up, enormous, implacable, demanding to be asked, and to be answered. There was no doubt about it: we'd have to take the bull by the horns.

I tried, though I instinctively found myself seeking to take the edge off the seriousness by laughing a little nervous laugh. I seem to remember quite a lot of coughs and splutters from Mark, too, before finally, grace abandoned me altogether and I launched in.

'Now, Stephanie, Gena's told us a bit about how you came to this decision to be a surrogate. Could you tell us in your own words?'

Her answer showed how much she'd thought it over. She

said, 'I've seen how happy Gena's become through having the chance to have John, and I'd like to make someone happy in that way, too. I feel I've been a selfish person for most of my life, and it's time I did something for somebody else. Nine months out of my life is a small sacrifice to make to give someone such happiness. You see, I've always lived surrounded by children, there are a lot in my family, and my Mum worked as a social worker in a children's home, where I used to go a lot to visit. So I've always loved children and had a great involvement with them, I know how important they are. I definitely want a family of my own when I find the right person. But I want to be a surrogate first, while I'm young. Then I'll have the rest of my life ahead of me in which to have my own children and do things for myself.'

It's always hard to accept that people can actually be doing things for others totally altruistically, with no ulterior motive – especially, maybe, if they're willing to do something you really want them to do for yourself. At various points during that afternoon, Mark and I put this same question to Stephanie again . . . and again – getting blunter with her about it every time. We quizzed her in the kitchen, when Gena wasn't around; we even took her outside to discuss her reasons, maybe feeling that if she literally came into the open, it would prompt her to do so verbally, too. It wasn't that we disbelieved her – no, we were impressed by her directness, her obvious sincerity. But it's so hard to know what is really in someone's heart, especially when you're meeting for the first time.

She never wavered from the gist of her original answer, however, and in the end we had to accept that we wanted the impossible: to know for sure why she was doing this. We'd never be inside her head, or know absolutely how she felt. As Gena had said, we'd have to trust her.

I was struck by the fact Stephanie said she cared so much about children and wanted her own. Naturally, I had to ask, 'How will you cope with giving up the baby?'

'I reckon I'll feel a mixture of things; I expect that in my own way, I will love the child, so there'll be a great sadness on parting. But if I'm going to do this, I'll consider it to be *your* child, not mine, and I know I'll have the strength to part with it because of how much happiness I'll be giving you. I'll feel sad in a way, but happy at the same time, you know, good about it in myself. And if I have support from you and very close friends, I'll cope.'

It was an answer that I suppose might have disconcerted some people, because it admitted the difficulties. But I felt humbled by her words; I realized that in a sense, it takes much more love to give up your child than to keep it. For us, Stephanie's reply was a lot more convincing than someone just swearing blind they wouldn't get involved with the baby at all and it would all be water off a duck's back. We returned to this question, too, several times, I guess to see if she had any hesitation, but she was always consistent about it. She might care for the baby, but it would be *ours*, and she would give it up to us, gladly, as that was what she wanted to do.

On the medical and practical sides, too, we really couldn't fault her answers – not that we wanted to, but I'm one of these people who gets a wee bit suspicious if things seem too perfect: I start to think it's all too good to be true.

Mark, reading my mind again, asked her, 'Aren't you worried about the risks involved in childbearing? I mean, you could die in childbirth, or end up having a hysterectomy . . . I'm sorry to sound so brutal . . . But we need to know *you* know these things.'

'That's okay, don't worry. I know about the risks, but after all, I could die just crossing the road right now, you know? Life is a risk, and this is something I want to do, so I'll have to accept the element of danger, but hope that I'm fit, healthy, and young, so things won't go wrong for me.'

Put baldly like this, maybe her answer sounds too simple: but it was said with such calm conviction, it just sounded sensible. And underlying each thing she said was the fact that she had made up her mind.

In relation to the medical aspect, she assured us she'd already taken great pains to contact her mother and father to check that there were no hereditary disorders in her family. They'd confirmed that over the past four or five generations – which was as far back as they knew – there was nothing of this nature, either mental or physical. She added that her mother had said she'd be prepared to answer any of our questions about this and give us more information if we wanted it.

We then asked Stephanie if, when she was scanned and tested in early pregnancy, it turned out the baby was seriously handicapped, she'd be prepared to have an abortion. She said yes, if that was what we wanted, because as far as she was concerned, though it was her body, it was our baby she'd be carrying, and we would have the right to decide on such matters. It was hardly a comfortable position for us, having to ask such things of someone we scarcely knew, but I had to remind myself that after all, I wasn't asking her to think of doing something I wouldn't have done myself in such a situation. I watched her like a hawk as she answered. I was unnerved by her calmness, yet at the same time I wished I could just accept it, and stop doubting her clear and considered answers.

We needed to know whether she was involved in a sexual relationship with anyone at present. She wasn't, and she wasn't on the Pill, or using a form of contraception such as the IUD (coil), which would have had to be removed before she began trying to conceive. We were very concerned to make sure that if we went ahead, the baby she had was definitely Mark's. Stephanie said she'd be perfectly willing to have a pregnancy test before we started trying, to show she wasn't already pregnant. Equally, she was happy for herself and the child to undergo the genetic fingerprint (DNA) blood test after the birth, which would show conclusively that it was Mark's baby. She said she was quite happy to abstain from sex altogether for the whole time we were trying to conceive, if that was what we wanted; and she already knew everything she had to do concerning monitoring her menstrual cycle, and inseminating herself.

When we heard that she wasn't involved with anyone, we immediately wanted to know how she would deal with being single and pregnant – what story she'd tell people once her pregnancy began to show, and if she was intending to have anyone around for moral support. She told us that for the duration of the pregnancy a very good friend of hers called

Richard was quite happy to pose as the baby's father if need be, and that he was prepared to give up his job to come and stay with her if she wanted him to. They had previously had a relationship, but were now just friends, though she thought they might possibly have a relationship again in future.

We were happy with this situation, because frankly, at this stage, we still didn't know whether, if we went ahead with surrogacy, it would be wise to become too close to the surrogate. This had nothing to do with how we felt about Stephanie; I'd have had the same attitude no matter who we were involved with. I was very wary of forming a bond with whoever it might be, just in case the worst came to the worst, and she refused to give up the baby. Though we already felt pretty sure of Stephanie in this regard, we also felt it would be better for her to have someone apart from us with whom she could share the whole experience; not just for her sake, I admit, but for ours as well. We didn't envisage becoming a substitute family for her while she was pregnant; in fact, we hadn't looked enough at the situation from her point of view, or thought how lonely and vulnerable she could become, away from her work and family, pregnant and in a strange town. At any rate, when we discussed the practicalities of what would happen if we went ahead, I said openly that I had grave doubts about becoming close to anyone in this sort of situation, and I'd even thought at one point of not meeting her at all!

As usual, Stephanie took it all in her stride, but rather surprised us by saying she thought it would be better if we had a fairly close relationship. She said quite definitely that this would help *her*, not just in giving her support, but also because she would know properly the people the baby would be going to and what sort of home it would grow up in, which would make it easier for her to give us the child. And she added that if we were in close contact, it would also give me a better chance to bond with the baby by sharing in the pregnancy.

Although I'd already said I wanted to be there at the birth, this last point hadn't occurred to me, and, for all my anxieties, I felt Stephanie was right. Though living nearby and seeing a lot of each other might bring a lot of stresses and responsibilities, on the other hand, we'd be able to see how everything was going – and be right there if anything went wrong. I asked Stephanie how she'd feel, if we decided to go ahead, about living at my mother's, if only temporarily. I said we didn't want to pressurize her, we'd arrange alternative accommodation if she preferred, but Mum's was near us and she'd be with someone she could get to know well. She readily agreed, and said she was eager to start everything as soon as possible. At this, I went off and rang my mother to see if we could bring Stephanie back with us to her place that night – *if* we chose to go on with the whole plan. Mum was rather shocked, but quite agreeable. She just reminded me to make sure in my own mind this was what I really wanted to do before we committed ourselves. Good old Mum!

Lastly, we discussed expenses with Stephanie, and reached an agreement on that. There seemed nothing left to talk about, at least for now: we'd fired questions at her left, right and centre almost non-stop for about two hours, and to every one, she'd provided a virtually perfect answer. She seemed happy enough with us: all that remained to do was for us to decide here and now whether we were going through with this or not. We knew there were many other couples waiting on Gena's list, and Stephanie was very keen to get on with things, so it was important to make the decision as soon as possible.

Mark and I told Gena and Stephanie we needed to go off for a while to talk it over on our own, so we set out for a walk. To begin with, neither of us said very much at all: each was watching the other for a reaction, as neither wanted to force the other's hand.

At last Mark said, 'Well? What d'you think?'

It turned out we felt much the same way. While we were worried about how young Stephanie was – in years at least – we were both very impressed, if not to say slightly shocked, by how forthright and definite she'd been – we'd never come across such a manner in a girl her age. But shocked or not, neither of us could deny that she knew exactly what she was about, and seemed totally determined.

79

Suddenly, at this moment, little John, Gena's son, ran up to join us, saying he wanted to walk, too. He took hold of one of each of our hands, and trotted happily between us, while we tried to continue our conversation above him, not quite sure how much he might or might not be taking in. I thought of his innocence, and of what we were discussing, and something about the situation touched me. In my mind I have a very clear image of that moment, the two of us walking in the late afternoon, with the little boy between us, and the decision biding its time.

Then, out of nowhere, fighter planes appeared, swooping in a glint of silver wings, trailing their thin streamers of sound. John was terrified, and in spite of assurances, ran back to the house as fast as his legs could carry him. As we resumed our walk, the fighters, too, were gone; once again we were alone in the sudden silence that followed their passing. The weight of our momentous decision seemed to hang above our heads in the empty air.

I said that I was ninety-nine percent sure – as sure as I could be until it happened – that Stephanie would give up the baby; and that even if she was very young, I was satisfied with her explanation of why she wanted to do this at this stage in her life, it made sense to me. Mark agreed, and said, 'Well, we could put off this decision for another six months or so, while we mull over the whole thing again: but what's to say we wouldn't then put it off *again*, and even if we said yes, in six months' time we wouldn't still have this opportunity. It seems to me we've made our decision: we're happy about surrogacy, we're as sure of Stephanie as we're going to be of anyone: it's really only our fear that's holding us back . . .'

I agreed, and added, 'We've done everything we can to cross-examine Gena and Stephanie; we've had all our questions answered. We can't really *think* any more about it – we've exhausted thinking. We've just got to take the plunge.'

He nodded. 'Yes. We've run out of excuses. This is it.'

And that was indeed that. We turned back from that walk with much trepidation, but also full of excitement. We'd made what was probably the biggest decision of our lives. As we came into Gena's sitting room, Stephanie looked up, the question in her eyes. I looked at her, and somehow, from somewhere, produced a nervous smile.

'Okay,' I said. 'Let's go.'

7
TRYING TIMES

When Stephanie moved into my mother's that night, her ovulation days for that month's cycle had just passed. We therefore had three or four weeks to wait before she'd be ovulating again and we could start on our first attempt to conceive. Though this was rather tantalizing, it gave us all time to get to know each other a bit better: during these weeks we went out for a drink a few times, and got on fine. Stephanie seemed a lot more talkative than on that first meeting, which took us a little by surprise, but we seemed to be doing all right.

Uppermost in all our minds really was sex – or, to be more precise, reproduction. A good deal of that time was spent making sure we had all the equipment we'd need for the insemination, and knew – if only in theory! – how to go about it.

Although the basic procedure was quite simple, there were lots of details to remember. As Gena had suggested, we bought, from a chemist, a digital thermometer and an ovulation kit for Stephanie to use so she'd know when she was ovulating. Using the kit involved Stephanie passing a urine sample when she was approaching the mid-point of her cycle, into which she would dip a sliver of specially-coated paper which changed colour slightly if she was about to ovulate. So that *we* would also be aware of this, Mark and I kept a chart recording each day, which meant we'd know roughly when to start abstaining from sex so that Mark's sperm count would be high when he produced the specimen for conception. Gena had given Stephanie the syringe – minus needle – which she would use to inseminate herself, and we supplied her with some tablets to make a sterile solution in which to immerse it, so it would be sterile when it came to filling it with semen. Apart from that, the only other equipment Stephanie needed was a pregnancy testing kit . . . and a lot of patience.

Meanwhile, for our part, it was mainly up to Mark – in fact, now I think of it, this was one of the few times in this whole caper when I had to take a back seat. Until now, I'd more or less arranged everything – after all, he was working, while I had been at home since my hysterectomy – but now he came into his own. We read a fair amount on the subject of infertility, in magazines such as those supplied by COTS and the National Association for the Childless (NAC), and discovered that it would improve our chances of conceiving if Mark wore baggy boxer shorts instead of his usual underwear (so his testicles weren't constricted). It was also apparently better for him to avoid travelling in any way that created a lot of vibration, as this affected the sperm's motility and potency – but, as he's a helicopter pilot, there wasn't an awful lot he could do about that!

The other main thing we learnt was that a better semen sample was produced if the man was very aroused before ejaculating, so Mark thought the best way to ensure this was for me to help him at the appointed moment. At the time, this seemed to make good sense, and anyway, I was happy to do whatever I could to help . . . at least, to begin with I was.

Sometime round the beginning of September, Mum rang to deliver the message we'd been waiting for.

'Rona, tell Mark to come over as soon as he can. Stephanie's going green!'

This cryptic code didn't actually mean Stephanie was seasick, or had suddenly become environmentally friendly: no, it was Mum's shorthand for telling us that the coated paper was turning dark green when Stephanie tested her urine, meaning she was ovulating.

This was it: the moment we'd all been looking forward to. As soon as Mark got back from work, I told him, 'She's going green, she's going green!'

Like me, he was delighted at the news. We were both

absolutely sure at that point that Stephanie would conceive first time, no question – after all, it seemed that girls were always getting pregnant accidentally, so surely, we reasoned, if we did everything at her most fertile time, she was *bound* to conceive. So now it was just a matter of getting the precious semen sample.

Full of excitement, I went and fetched our version of a specimen jar – in reality, an old empty aspirin bottle we'd cleaned out and sterilized in boiling water – and we made our way into the bedroom. We'd been dutifully chaste for a good week by now, and we both felt deeply moved at the thought that we were going to be conceiving our child, so we were looking forward to this in every way. It seemed a very serious, romantic moment, all very lovey-dovey . . .

Until, that is, we reached the climactic point. Surely nothing can switch so quickly from the sublime to the ridiculous as sex. There we were, stark naked on the bed, with Mark in a state of undisguised excitement. I reached for the empty aspirin bottle, and sat up. This wasn't a new version of 'Not tonight, darling, I've got a headache', but rather, the next step in the plan: somehow to get what was inside Mark outside, and straight into the bottle. And now things began to get complicated. Excitement gave way to confusion: like a variation on a scene of first love, we sat on the bed together, with me clutching the aspirin (and aspiring) jar, looking at each other and wondering, 'What happens next?'

What did happen next would have provided a fair bit of hilarity for anyone listening at the door. It would have sounded something like this:

A few seconds of speculative silence. Then:
ME (solemnly): 'Now, are you going to manage to control it and make it go in there?'
Inaudible response.
Silence.
ME (anxiously): 'No, no, keep it still! You've got it at the wrong angle!'
Slight silence.
HE (urgently): 'No, no, get the pot nearer!'

HE (frantically): 'Now! Now! Put the pot on the end! . . .'
Fumbling noises.
BOTH TOGETHER (dismayed): 'No! No! OH NO!'
Stunned pause.
HE (pensively): 'How was it for you, darling?'

I fell back on the bed, shaking with helpless laughter. I thought 'This is *unreal*, I don't believe we're doing this!' Mark, laughing also, and now rather less excited, stood in the middle of the room, holding the jar and trying not to spill any of the few sacred drops that had actually found their way in there – for most of the 'sample' seemed to be spread round the rest of the room.

Once our hilarity had subsided, we hurriedly dressed and jumped in the car for the high-speed 'emergency' dash to Mum's, to deliver the goods. Not to put too fine a point on it, it was important that the semen should be as fresh as possible for the insemination, and it also had to be kept at body temperature, which meant Mark had to tuck the bottle somewhere exciting such as under his armpit, into his trouser pocket or down his underpants. Keeping it warm meant the semen would become runny, losing its glutinous consistency, so it would be easier for Stephanie to draw into and express out of the syringe, and it also reduced the number of sperm that died off.

When we'd safely handed over the sample, such as it was, there was nothing left to do but sit and have a cup of tea while Stephanie inseminated herself upstairs. To do this, she decanted the semen from the pot into the syringe, then lay on her bed with her bottom slightly raised on a couple of pillows, inserted the syringe into her vagina, expressed the semen into herself, and removed the empty syringe. She then had to stay lying down for at least an hour to stop the semen from flowing out again and give the sperm time to swim up into her uterus and fallopian tubes, where, hopefully, they'd meet the egg somewhere along the way and fertilize it.

We'd agreed it would be best to try two or even three times at each ovulation, and the pattern we followed was to produce specimens on the first, third, and maybe fifth days of the 'going green' phase, with a rest on the second and fourth days. So a couple of days after the very first try, Mark and I again found ourselves in the bedroom with the aspirin bottle.

It soon became clear we weren't going to get very far with this technique. I just couldn't stop laughing, and once I started, no matter how hard he tried, it became impossible for Mark to keep a straight face – or anything else. But we still needed to get that sample. After a while we decided the best thing would be for Mark to buy a girlie magazine and just do what he had to do by himself. We also worked out that if he could produce the goods actually at Mum's, in her bathroom, say, it would save him having to do the high-speed drive with the sample down his trousers.

There was one thing bothering Mark about this, however. As we drove round to Mum's that evening, girlie magazine at the ready, he said, 'It might be a good idea if you could get me warmed up now, while we're *en route*. That way, I'll be pretty excited by the time I start on the magazine, and I'll probably produce a better sample. You know they said arousal's important.'

At the time, I thought he was just winding me up, trying to get a bit of fun out of me: after all, although it had been quite a novelty, getting the specimen was hardly galvanizing our sex life into a new gear, and what with abstaining for five days beforehand, and (apart from the 'sperm retrieval' efforts) for the ovulation week as well, we were having a fairly dull time of it. So I played along with this idea, for the moment anyway, but only in a very half-hearted way. Mark soon noticed I wasn't very enthusiastic, and, one day, he suddenly stopped the car and explained to me, syllable by syllable, that I was going to have to do my share of the work, it wasn't fair to expect him to do it all on his own, and anyhow he needed to be highly excited to increase the amount of sperm he produced, it was as simple as that. This was the bottom line.

I realized he meant what he said, and took the hint. And so it was that two or three times a month, we'd find ourselves driving along, with me keeping Mark amused, and him trying to concentrate on the road and the job at the same time. We never had an accident, either with the driving or the other business, but we did once have to call a hasty halt to our activities when Mark happened to notice a police car cruising along behind us. And once or twice we nearly forgot to stop our antics in plenty of time before parking, and Mark was almost caught literally with his trousers down by unsuspecting passers-by.

He had quite a hard time of it, I suppose. As soon as Mum opened the door and saw the state of him, she'd burst out laughing, which hardly boosted his ego; and then it was upstairs with him, banished into the bathroom to do his business. At that time, this room hadn't been redecorated, so Mark had to sit there with his togs off, trying to work himself into an erotic lather over his magazine, while freezing gales rushed up through the gaps in the bare wooden floorboards.

It was small wonder that, as time went on, he wanted to get it over as quickly as possible, and managed to get the whole thing down to a fine art. Mum and I always used to wait downstairs and make some tea while he got on with it; and gradually, we noticed that whereas in the early days, we'd have plenty of time to put the kettle on, wait for it to boil, fill the cups and go through to the lounge before he returned, instead, as the months wore on, we'd find the kettle had barely started to steam before he'd be walking in the kitchen, sample secured and already passed to Stephanie for 'processing'. In fact towards the end of this time of trying, he started to joke that it wouldn't be long before he was so conditioned he'd just have to hear the click of the kettle switch being pressed and 'Hey presto!' he'd have the sample.

For all this surface hilarity, however, underneath, we were all feeling the strain. From Mark's and my point of view, there were a number of factors that were making life extremely stressful during those months between September 1988 and the early part of the New Year. To begin with, once the novelty wore off, trying to conceive meant a drastic change in our sex life. Each month, the period of joint abstinence would be followed by about a week in which we had to make do with the somewhat tantalizing sessions in the car, and, for Mark, a couple of 'sperm retrieval' efforts alone in Mum's bathroom – hardly what could pass for a Festival of Erotica. Then, when Stephanie had passed the ovulation stage, we were able to resume normal marital affairs for about a fortnight – or that was the theory. In practice though, even this time was constrained by the discipline of the rest of the month's proceedings. It never actually got to the point where I had to wrap myself in a white cloth with 'Aspirin' written on it in order to get Mark excited, but there were times when spontaneity seemed to have gone right out of the window; we'd find ourselves saying, 'Well, we'd better have sex tonight, because we won't be able to have it for another ten days.' Somehow, planned sex just didn't feel the same, and it was hard to come to terms with this strange change in our relationship: surrogacy seemed to be encroaching on the most private areas of our lives in an unnervingly relentless way.

I say that, yet one of the worst problems I had to face during this period was the fact that finding Stephanie, and trying for a baby, *hadn't* resolved my acute sense of grief and loss about everything that had happened in May. Of course, I felt hope and excitement at the thought that we might conceive a child with Stephanie; but deep down, it was as if nothing had changed. I couldn't seem to get over what had happened, I still relived it over and over, both by day and in my recurrent dream about the birth. To make matter worse, I felt now, four or five months after the event, as if people expected me to have recovered, and this made me feel bad, abnormal and guilty that I was still grieving. I felt I was a burden on people, and that maybe I should have pulled myself out of this by now.

Eventually, I went to see my doctor about it. I told him I couldn't seem to get on with my life, I couldn't concentrate on anything for any length of time, I seemed to be always in the depths of depression, crying, and so on. He was very sympathetic, and said that this whole experience was like a

Mark and me on our wedding day, 18 May 1988.

Kathleen soon after she was born, 5 November 1989.

Me holding Kathleen an hour after her birth, with Stephanie looking on.

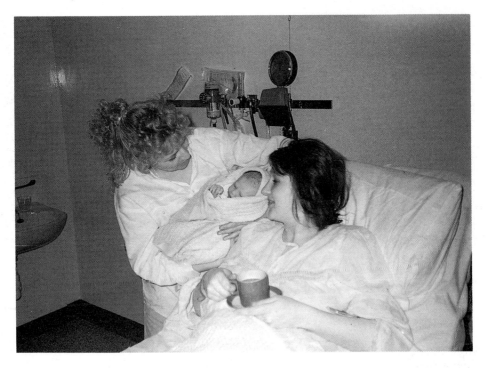

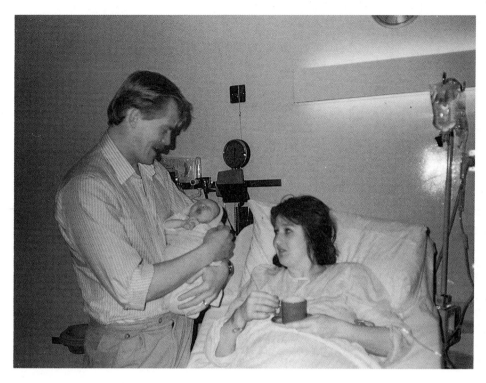

Mark holding Kathleen, at Stephanie's bedside.

The day after the birth. Stephanie, Richard, Megan and Mum with Kathleen.

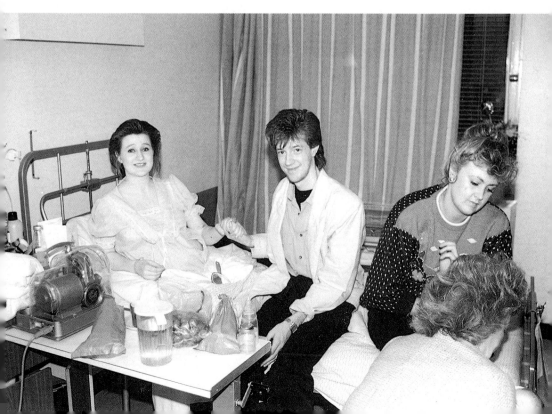

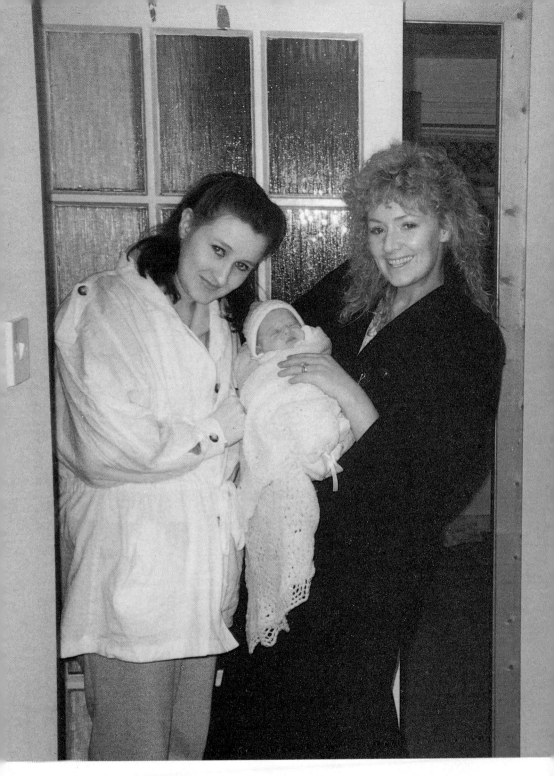

Arriving at the cottage, Stephanie hands Kathleen over to me.

Mum sees her granddaughter
for the first time, 6 November
1989.

My sister, Megan, holding
Kathleen a week after her
birth.

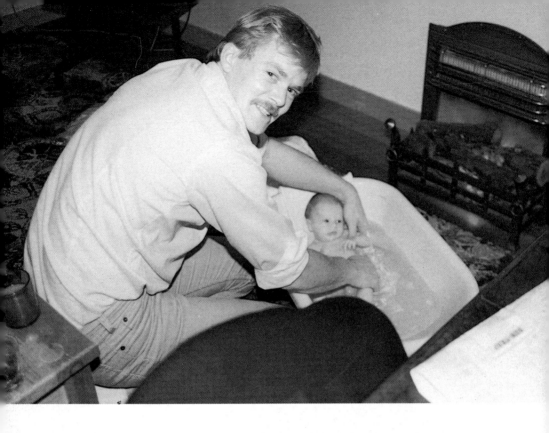

Me and Mark bathing Kathleen at the cottage, when she was a week old.

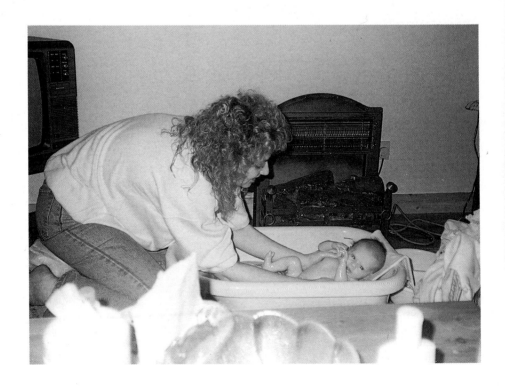

Taking Kathleen for her first walk.

The three of us at home, February 1990.

bend in my life that right now I was stuck on, but that if I could once get past it, round the corner as it were, life would start to progress. He suggested having counselling, which at the time I didn't want; then he advised taking a holiday that would force me to do something different, and take me into a new environment. Following this advice, Mark and I went to Rhodes, with my sister and her fiancé. It certainly helped to prise me out of the vicious circle I was in, at least for a while. But it was to be many more months before I really did break free, and worked my way out of that terrible tunnel of deep grieving and into the light. And, in the meantime, there were other clouds hanging over us.

Things with Stephanie were not going well. Originally, when we'd first considered surrogacy, we'd thought our greatest problems and fears would come during the time of the birth onwards, when we'd have to deal with the social services. But in fact a lot of the worries were coming up during this time of trying to conceive, and getting to know Stephanie, and attempting to sort out our own life and feelings around that. Basically, we were now beginning to understand what we'd let ourselves in for by embarking on surrogacy. The truth was, if Stephanie was having a baby for us, we were going to be involved with her whether we liked it or not: and unfortunately, during this phase, we *didn't* like it. Although we'd agreed to keep in close contact, since this was what she wanted and seemed to need, I'm afraid Mark and I found this heavy going. I wish I could have known then what I know now, and found it in myself to trust her more from the beginning, but the fact is, at this stage I was still too scared of letting myself go with her. Though I was as sure as I could be that she'd give up the baby, I just couldn't take any chances, as I was still too raw from what had happened to allow myself to get close to someone who might end up hurting me terribly. And, as Mark reasoned, it might not in any case be a good idea for us to become too intimate, because we'd agreed that after the birth it would be best for everyone if we all went our separate ways, and severed all links. If we now formed a strong bond, the parting would be very traumatic and we would all suffer. So we both kept a bit aloof from Stephanie at this time, which didn't make things any easier, and was maybe unfair on her, considering what we'd originally agreed.

The trouble was that even with the best will in the world, we didn't have a lot in common. The age gap between us was certainly a bit of a problem: but even when I'd been nineteen myself, I just hadn't been like her, so I found it even harder to accept some of her behaviour. As we got to know her better, we discovered she hardly seemed to stop chatting; and a few of the things she said seemed quite daft to me, just as I'm sure a lot of the things I talked about bored her stiff. She was always talking about herself – some days it just seemed her conversation was on one note, 'I' 'I' 'I' 'I' 'I' 'I' 'I' all the time, till I thought I'd scream if she said it once more. She seemed to say things one minute and contradict herself the next, which meant I never really knew why she'd said something in the first place, and if I pointed out her inconsistencies, she'd talk herself out of them – she could talk her way out of a paper bag, could Stephanie. She seemed pretty volatile in her moods as well, blowing hot and cold.

The problem was that I really didn't understand her at that time, and Mark and I just hadn't thought enough about her side of the situation. It was only much later that I understood that underneath her apparent confidence, her conceit even, she actually had a very low opinion of herself. But all this I only came to see through experience: during these early months, I didn't know any of it, and, ashamed though I am to admit it now, I actually disliked her. Though I didn't wish we'd never met, I started to think we'd made a mistake in taking on as a surrogate someone who needed so much support, who wasn't married or had children, or a family relationship of her own 'on tap', separate from ours.

So, when Richard came on the scene, about two months after we'd started trying for a baby, Mark and I were quite relieved in a way, as he was already a very good friend of Stephanie's and we felt he'd give her support. We liked him, he seemed a nice, easy-going, cheerful sort of chap, and, as we were soon to discover, he was devoted to Stephanie. However, my relief at him being around was mixed with some resentment and anxiety. I knew their relationship wasn't sexual at that time, but I was worried it might become so (as in fact it did), and we'd then have yet another complication in a situation which was already quite tortuous enough: when Stephanie became pregnant, we'd have to worry about whether the baby was Mark's or Richard's. But I told myself I musn't be selfish, it would be good for Stephanie to have Richard around, and after all, it was important for her to be happy.

But the point was that after a short while she *didn't* seem to be happy with him – quite the reverse in fact. For some reason, she started to treat him in an abominable fashion – so badly, I don't understand to this day why he stayed. He had moved into Mum's as well – to a different room – and initially, Mum didn't mind; she'd thrown herself heart and soul into helping us have this baby, and she understood implicitly how important it was to keep the peace by making Stephanie as happy as possible. Everything went along fine at first. But then, Stephanie began to go for Richard: she'd scream and shout, and throw things at him, telling him to get out of her life, to leave her alone and go back home. She didn't care what she did. Mum was often forced to intervene, to calm her down, but for months, Stephanie continued to treat Richard in a despicable way, so much so, that we felt sorry for him, staying and suffering it all so patiently. Ages afterward, Stephanie told me that later, when she'd asked him why he'd put up with her behaving so badly, he'd simply said he knew all along that she needed him. He was right. Maybe he also saw what we didn't see at the time, being so involved with our own worries: that, underneath her determined, confident exterior, Stephanie too was becoming impatient and anxious, and starting to feel inadequate – as indeed, to some extent, we all were.

For my part, I felt increasingly that I couldn't deal with Stephanie and Richard: it seemed to me that with them it was constant want, want, want, and complaint, complaint, complaint; they were always moaning. I suggested they move out of Mum's, thinking that maybe this might be part of the problem; but no, Stephanie didn't want that, she was attached to my mother, and I think enjoyed her company, and the support and attention she got from her. But the complaints went on. Eventually, one day, around December of that year, things came to a head. Richard rang me – he often seemed to act as 'spokesman' for them both – and started asking whether it would be possible for us to help them out with something; I can't now remember exactly what. As usual, they were having a hard time of it, or so he implied. I listened for a while to this tale of woe, and then something in me snapped. Without really thinking of the implications of my words, I said, 'Look, Richard, if you and Stephanie don't think you can handle this situation, and get yourselves together, then *I* can't handle it. I can't keep up with all the requests and complaints and the needs; I can't cope with it any longer. I've just had enough, and I think it's possibly better if Stephanie goes back home and finds somebody else, another couple, because I just don't think this is going to work. I can't take it any more. I've come to the end of the road.'

Though I'd just spoken completely spontaneously, without any particular plan – I was simply reacting – this little speech had an electrifying effect. Richard immediately started to backtrack like crazy, and protest that no, everything was okay; then Stephanie came on the 'phone, and said he'd exaggerated, they were fine really. So we managed to smooth it over, though afterwards, I felt awful about what I'd said, because though I'd meant every syllable, at the same time I didn't want to give up on surrogacy. But I'd never imagined we'd have so many problems with the surrogate at this stage. I hadn't thought we'd have to be so close, so at the mercy of her whims and emotions. Above all, I'd never dreamt that conception would take so long.

For this was the major problem on top of all the others: the months were trickling by, and still Stephanie wasn't pregnant. To make things worse, it took quite a while before our early optimism that she'd conceive straight away began to die down; so, for about four months, each time, we'd have this terrific excitement for most of the month, and then a tremendous let-down when her period came. Because we were all so eager for her to be pregnant, we didn't want to wait until her period was due each time before finding out, so we'd buy a pregnancy test and do it before then – and of course, with self-testing, there's always room for mistakes or misinterpretation of colour. So a couple of times, when we did the test, one or other of us would think it had gone blue, when in reality it hadn't, and we'd have to do it again, and of course it then came up negative. Under this kind of pressure, it was hardly surprising that Stephanie herself once or twice started to feel sure she was pregnant, and would say so; but, feeling or no feeling, relentlessly, punctually, her period would turn up just the same and drown all our hopes.

These frustrations were compounded by torments that in spite of all our preparation and zeal, we might be doing something wrong – as indeed we were on a couple of occasions. Like the pregnancy tests, but more so, the colour in the ovulation kits was quite difficult to gauge, and there were times when we'd be waiting and waiting for the special paper strip to show up the darkest green, to be sure Stephanie was ovulating (although the instructions *told* one the darkest shade might never be reached . . .), only to find her test didn't register any darker that month and would come up white a day later, showing we'd missed her most fertile time, she'd been the darkest she was going to be yesterday, or the day before. It was hell.

Knowing we could waste opportunities so easily, however vigilant we were, as time went on we did begin to wonder if we were doing other things wrong. And because Mark and I knew exactly what *we* were doing, in terms of the practical process we went through each month, and felt this was all watertight, we naturally started to worry that Stephanie was making a mistake somewhere along the line. We were fairly sure she couldn't be, but there was this little twinge of doubt, because it was the one part of the business we couldn't control. I must say here that, in spite of all the difficulties we had with her, Stephanie still had the most co-operative attitude towards the actual practice of surrogacy that any couple could wish for. She'd asked me at the start if I wanted to be with her when she inseminated herself, but I felt strongly that she must be allowed some privacy and leeway, we had to trust her, and I couldn't be standing over her in the bedroom to make sure she was doing things properly. Nevertheless, this meant we now fretted about it, knowing as we did that she wasn't always consistent about such things as taking her temperature at the same time each day.

On top of this, Stephanie's relationship with Richard gradually did develop into a sexual one, which brought other anxieties – not just about the paternity issue, but also about whether their sex-life might affect *our* chances of making her pregnant. When she told us she and Richard were having sex, I'd drilled and grilled her about using contraception – namely condoms – warning her of the wicked ways of sperms, that the little devils could crawl in the bed and so on, and that she must be super-careful: which she and Richard were. But this itself presented a problem, which only occurred to Mark and me sometime later. By this stage, we were avidly reading articles about ways to improve our chances of conceiving, and we'd come across one that suggested it was best if the woman, too, was aroused during insemination, because this meant the cervix opened slightly, increasing the sperms' chances of getting through into the womb.

We told Stephanie this, and eventually, she got Richard to help her – as Mark accidentally discovered.

It was a sperm retrieval day, and he'd seen Stephanie and Richard chatting together just before he went into the bathroom to do what he had to do. He was pretty quick about it these days, and it wasn't long before he was knocking on Stephanie's door, aspirin pot in hand. To his surprise, when he went in, Richard was nowhere to be seen, and Stephanie said rather breathlessly 'Oh, that was quick, I didn't think you'd be here so soon, I thought it must be Rona's mum knocking.'

Then she called, 'It's all right, Richard, it's only Mark, you can come out now!'

At which point the wardrobe door opened and out came

Richard, wearing nothing but a slightly sheepish grin. They explained that they'd been going to try and start intercourse, to get Stephanie excited before she inseminated herself.

Mark, though barely able to keep a straight face, managed to say, 'Well, I hope you were going to use a condom.' Then, as he said it, and they said yes, he realized the implications of this and exclaimed, 'Hang on a minute, condoms are coated in spermicide – this could kill off the sperm in my sample!'

In fact, on this occasion, there was nothing to worry about, for, as Richard rather blushingly admitted, he hadn't been able to get excited 'to order' anyway, so they hadn't got very far . . . We all had a good giggle about it at the time, but it just showed what a business it all was; a no-win situation if ever there was one.

Of course, we might have saved ourselves a lot of this trouble if we'd resorted to the natural method of conception, and Mark and Stephanie had had purely functional intercourse – if such a thing exists – instead of having to mess about with magazines, aspirin bottles and syringes. But I'd always felt I could never handle this, and had made this plain at the very start; and Stephanie, too, was adamant she couldn't and wouldn't do this.

All the same, as the fruitless months wore on, unbeknown to me, Mark began to debate with himself whether he shouldn't try to approach Stephanie without telling me, to see if she'd agree to attempt it. As he says now, it certainly wasn't what he wanted; but we were determined to have a baby, and as he saw it, the simple fact was that the natural method had evolved as it had because it was the most effective way of conceiving. Luckily, he did confide in his brother, Paul, about it, and one day when Mark was at work, Paul sounded me out on the subject – never saying that Mark was seriously considering it, but just wondering if I'd thought any more of it. As he put it, Mark and Stephanie could have found a way to keep it all as clinical and anonymous as possible – put pillows over each other's heads, I think was one ingenious idea.

My reaction was immediate and unambiguous. 'NO! NO! Shut up! I don't even want to think about it!' The very idea was horror of horrors to both myself and Stephanie – as I guess Paul now realized.

For after that, nothing more was heard – let alone done – about this little plan.

Though I was reacting mainly on instinct, I'm sure I was right to rule this out totally. While it might – and only *might* – have produced quicker results, I'm sure it would have had a disastrous effect on our marriage, whether or not Mark had managed to keep it a secret from me – which I very much doubt he could have done. If I hadn't known, there would always have been that shadow between us that he couldn't share and that I might discover, and if I *had*, I could never have got the thought out of my mind.

So that was no-go: and so, as it turned out, was any notion we might have entertained of possibly trying another surrogate. We'd all agreed at the start that we would try for as long as it took – thinking then that Stephanie would be pregnant at the drop of a hat – so to this extent we did feel under an obligation to her. But after five months or so of failed attempts, we were beginning to despair. Stephanie was very young, and theoretically at a very fertile stage in her life; and we knew Mark was fertile, since he'd already fathered our child. If Stephanie wasn't conceiving, there had to be a reason, and we couldn't help wondering if either she was infertile, or if there was what's known as 'unexplained infertility' between herself and Mark – that is, they'd each be able to conceive if partnered with somebody else, but together, the particular combination of his sperm and her egg was just incompatible. If this were the case, we felt we had to start considering other surrogates – there was never any question we'd give up altogether – but this created a crisis. We couldn't advertize for anyone; there was nobody who was both suitable and willing in either of our families; and, when I rang Gena confidentially, she said it was really out of the question. The only other potential surrogate currently around was totally unsuited to us physically, and anyway, there was nothing yet to show Stephanie actually was infertile. I knew this already, but now I'd begun to think it was never going to happen, we weren't going to have this baby after all, or at least, not with Stephanie.

I used to walk up and down the street, and if I saw a likely-looking girl, I'd actually start thinking to myself whether we could somehow approach her about it; but of course you can't just go out and ask someone out of the blue how they'd like to become a surrogate mother. I knew I was daft even to think of it, but I was now totally despondent. We'd already investigated all the other avenues; Stephanie was our last resort, and the last resort wasn't working.

One day I read an article in the latest COTS newsletter about a surrogate who'd just had a baby. She described how she'd never assumed she'd conceive straight away, and then it had worked first time. I thought, 'Oh, worked first time . . .' – and burst into tears. It seemed the last straw, like some kind of horrible little morality tale, 'Don't get your hopes up and you won't be disappointed . . .'

Finally, Mark and I decided we'd have to have an informed opinion about it all, so we consulted Susan, the friend who'd been so helpful when we were first considering surrogacy. As before, it was a great relief to see her. I hadn't truly acknowledged how pent-up and wretched I was until that moment.

Susan greeted us with a cheerful, 'Hello! How are you doing?'

Automatically, I started to say, 'Oh, we're fine, doing fine . . .' Then the sight of her concerned face, looking to see how she could help, cut right through me and I dissolved, crying, 'No, no, we're NOT!'

Once again, she came to the rescue. She worked in an infertility clinic, and when she heard how we'd been carrying on, she told us we were being far too zealous, trying too many times each month, instead of concentrating on getting exactly the right moment.

'At the clinic we only try once every month, but we make sure we get the right time. Timing is everything in these matters.'

She added that we should buy our ovulation kits from the hospital, which sold its own type of kit to the public;

these were far more accurate than the shop-bought varieties, because you simply had to watch for *any* change in colour, not for a deepening shade of the same basic green.

'As soon as it shows any change at all, that's it, she's ovulating; the hormone level is rising, you must inseminate.'

Susan also said that, having heard our story, and the way we were feeling, she thought we should just try once or twice more, with the new kit, and if we still didn't have any luck, give it a rest for six months or so. We needed to take time away from all this and get our spirits back up, and break the tension that had built up between all of us. Then perhaps we could try again.

Her advice was just the boost we needed. We came away feeling a bit more positive. We had the new ovulation kit; and we'd also discovered a couple of extra tips ourselves, which we decided to try. One was something Gena had told us about the efforts of another pilot and his wife to conceive. His clinic had suggested he could boost his sperm count by having a cold shower, then lying naked flat on a bed in a cool atmosphere for about an hour before ejaculation. The other tip I think came from the NAC magazine, and advised not using the last part of the ejaculation as a sample, since the healthiest sperm were contained in the first part.

So the end of January 1989 came round. We gathered ourselves for what we knew might be our last attempt, at least for a while – although we hadn't said anything to Stephanie about this, thinking we'd wait and see how this effort went before we made our decision. Stephanie and Richard in fact seemed to be getting on a bit better with each other; and they'd agreed it would be best all round if they moved out to a place of their own. They were due to go to a mobile home a few miles from town in a couple of weeks. Stephanie seemed optimistic about this month's attempt; she'd read her horoscope in *The Sun* that week, which had promised great things in store. She'd decided this meant she'd get pregnant. I suppose I should have shared her enthusiasm; even though I'd no faith whatever in the predictions of a tabloid newspaper, Mark and I had actually got those more practical reasons to hope for success. But we knew we could only try once this month, not just because of Susan's advice, but because Mark was booked to be away for part of the time when Stephanie might be ovulating; and I felt it was very unlikely that the one try now would do the trick. Frankly, I'd decided it wasn't ever going to work. I felt that Someone Up There didn't want us to have a baby, and it wasn't to be, not for us at any rate.

Nevertheless, Stephanie used the new ovulation kit, and at the first fluctuation in colour, Mark sprang into the shower, drenched himself in cold water, and then, the January weather notwithstanding, lay down flat on the bed, starkers, with the window wide open, freezing himself for an hour before whizzing over for his sperm session. Then he set off for his time away, both of us trying not to think about what might or might not be happening inside Stephanie's body.

A few weeks later, Mark and I drove out to have a meal with Stephanie and Richard in their new home – as we thought, to have a drink and celebrate the move. When we got there, I immediately noticed that Stephanie was shaking slightly, so I knew there was something up; but I also knew it was a few days before her period was due, so it couldn't be anything to do with 'the business'. Anyway, I reminded myself firmly, 'that's not going to happen, don't you go getting your hopes up again.'

We sat there with our drinks for about half an hour, chatting about this and that, and then all of a sudden Stephanie just spurted out, 'I think I'm pregnant!'

Before we could say anything, she rushed off into the other room and came running back with a jar in her hand crying, 'What d'you think, do you think this is blue, do you think this is blue?' – then brandished it up to the light for us to see.

And there it was. This time, there could be no mistaking the colour that shone through the glass. It was a bright, bright, most brilliant blue.

8
PREGNANCY

The pregnancy was confirmed by the doctor about a week later. Our excitement was matched only by our enormous sense of relief – it was as if a great burden had been lifted from our shoulders. Stephanie, too, was over the moon, and seemed to be in much better spirits. Suddenly, life seemed transformed: we could forget the awful strain of the past months when we thought of the joy to come. It was such a luxury for us all to be able to look forward again, instead of brooding over each barren day. It really was going to happen. At last, on 29 October – or thereabouts! – we would have a baby.

Our relief lasted precisely one week. Then, one day when Mark was out, the phone rang.

As I answered it, a female voice I'd never heard before said, 'Hi, this is Stephanie, how're you doing?'

My heart seemed to seize up with panic. I said, 'I'm sorry, but this isn't Stephanie . . . Who *are* you? What's going on?'

She replied, 'You don't know me, my name's Joyce, I'm a friend of Stephanie's from the caravan site, and I'm phoning because I think it's only fair you should know that Stephanie has been telling people at the site all about your arrangements behind your back. You obviously have a lot of trust in your relationship with her and I think you should be aware that that trust has been betrayed.'

I felt icy cold, terrified. But I didn't dare say anything about what she'd just told me, since I didn't know how much *she* really did or didn't know, whether this was some sort of horrible tasteless joke.

I asked, 'How did you get my number?'

'I was in the phone box with Stephanie when she rang the

doctor for the results of the pregnancy test. Then she rang you and reversed the charges.'

This was true. The woman went on remorselessly, 'I know everything that's happened. Your husband's a pilot, his name's Mark, you can't have children, so Stephanie is going to have a baby for you, she's been artificially inseminating herself with Mark's sperm every month using a syringe.'

She carried on, detailing the practical process we'd been following. Then she added that Stephanie was making trouble, so she (Joyce) had been to tell the landlord at the site what was going on, he wasn't happy about it, and maybe I'd better contact him.

I couldn't believe this woman was on the end of the phone to me, that this had actually happened. Of course, I knew from Gena and from press articles that now and again there were disasters, somebody outside did get to know and the cover got blown, but it was such an awful thing to contemplate I guess I'd just tried to put it out of my mind. And anyway, we'd agreed to maximum secrecy at the start, and we'd been so careful. Or Mark and I had been.

When Joyce had finished her grim little tale, I stood for some seconds in stricken silence. I couldn't think what to do, but I had to stop this *now*.

Eventually I said very quickly and quietly, 'Look, what you're saying may be true, but it's something we're no longer taking part in. Whatever we may have thought of doing about surrogacy in the past is no longer relevant, as we're not going ahead. So will you please now just keep quiet and leave us alone.'

I was sure she didn't believe me, but I didn't give her a chance to say so. I hung up. I was so distressed, I immediately broke down. Through my tears, feeling utterly sick at heart, I tried to work out what was best to do. The girl had said she was calling to alert us: she'd never mentioned hush money or anything like that, and though it seemed to me a strange thing to do, to phone a total stranger, somehow she'd sounded very persuasive and sincere, and not at all vindictive, and I believed she probably wasn't trying to blackmail us. But if *she* knew, and the landlord knew, how many other people did? I had to get hold of Stephanie right away – apart from anything else, I had to get to the bottom of this, and have it out with her. I could hardly credit it, that here we were one week into this pregnancy and already this had happened, she was spreading the news around. But how else could Joyce have known every detail? My panic was fast giving way to fury. How could Stephanie have done this to us, how *could* she? Well, I was going to sort her out.

The trouble was, she and Richard had no telephone in the mobile home, so I had to ring Richard at work – he'd got himself a job to help support them during this time – and get him to tell Stephanie to ring me. Then I rang Gena. I was pretty much beside myself by this time. Having outlined what had happened I just cried, 'Get Stephanie out of there! Do something! This is all about to blow up!'

Gena was dismayed, and promised to call the landlord of the site to tell him to get Stephanie to contact me urgently – I needed Gena to do this so my line could stay clear, in case Richard had managed to reach Stephanie and she was already trying to ring in.

There followed a miserable two hours in which I watched and waited and worked myself into a rage, wondering what sort of story Stephanie was concocting during this delay. That sounds horrible, but I was shocked by how much Joyce knew, and stunned by the fact she knew anything at all. And, I thought bitterly, if *this* had already happened now, so early on, what on earth was the rest of the pregnancy going to be like? Were we in for nine months of sheer hell?

Finally, Stephanie rang. She said that she and Joyce had been friends, but had fallen out. Joyce wasn't really in her right mind, she was in the care of a social worker at the moment; anyway, one day after their bust-up, Joyce had gone into Stephanie's bedroom while Stephanie was having a bath, and rifled through all her papers, letters and diary, and that was how she'd gleaned all the inform- ation, including my phone number, which was written in the diary.

I said 'Okay, but then how did she know that you called

the doctor and then immediately called me and reversed the charges?'

'Well, in my diary I keep a note of all my calls to you, I write down "Called Rona (reversed charges)".'

'I see. Right.'

I didn't believe her. Mentally unstable or not, Joyce had known far too many details to have possibly deduced it all from letters in the time it took Stephanie to have a bath. But Stephanie was adamant, and there was nothing I could do to prove or disprove her story. All that seemed left to do was to make sure it never happened again, and, if possible, to get Stephanie off the site at once.

I said, 'Right. The bottom line is that you should never have our number written down in your book, and if you *must* have anything down in writing, lock it away, don't leave it lying around where anyone can wander in and find it.'

'But I shouldn't have to do that – she's to blame, she's ruining everything. Now I won't be able to keep any letters, I'll have to rip them up . . .'

'Look, Stephanie, we're a week into this, and *this* has happened: this is a major disaster.' And I told her I thought they'd better move.

But, as usual, she had an answer to that as well. She said that if she and Richard did that, everyone at the site would know the story Joyce had told was true, they'd say they'd got the better of her and she'd left, which was just what they wanted. The landlord had already told her he didn't care what she did behind closed doors, but his was a quiet, respectable site, and if there was one sniff of the press coming round, she'd be straight out, no notice, nothing.

I could see Stephanie's point; and she was so determined not to leave, it was soon clear I'd be wasting my breath trying to argue with her. So in the end I said she had to be very careful in picking her friends, it was no good telling people she'd only known for a few weeks, and especially if they were also possibly unstable and under the control of the social services! She reiterated that she hadn't told Joyce.

'Well, this must *never* happen again. Don't write things

down, and delete our name and number from your book –
understood?'

My anger was plain. Stephanie did something she didn't
normally do – she was silent on the end of the line for a
while. Then she said she was as upset as we were about it.

As things turned out, it all blew over – though Joyce rang
me three more times in the next four days, before we changed
our number and shook her off that way. Quite how Stephanie
and Richard faced it out on the site I'll never know – nor
exactly what the truth of the matter was. It left a bad taste
in my mouth for quite some time afterward. Our confidence
was shaken, and we felt in spite of all the time we'd put in
over the past six months, we'd just stepped into the unknown
and were in for a pretty rough ride over the next nine. To be
quite honest, had Stephanie not been pregnant, I think we'd
have called it a day there and then. As it was, that was out of
the question. We were trapped – or so it seemed at that time:
that's how bad it was. The only useful lesson to come out of
it all was just how important it was to be careful not to let
slip one word about what we were doing to anyone outside
our immediate family, and a very few intimate friends. But
we knew this already, and frankly, we'd rather have been
reminded of it some other less traumatic way.

I dearly wish I could say that our relationship with Stephanie
improved soon after this – that, in spite of this setback,
the fact she was pregnant with our child brought us all
closer together. But this just wasn't the case, not in these
early months anyway. Certainly, her pregnancy did make
a difference, and it may well have had a big impact on
Stephanie herself, because around this time her relationship
with Richard underwent a dramatic change. Almost overnight, she stopped attacking and abusing him, and seemed
to relax more. She became calmer. It was as if she'd made
up her mind about him once and for all; they were together,
settled.

So, in that sense, she seemed happier. But from our point
of view, the relationship with her remained uneasy; in fact,
though we were over the moon about her being pregnant,

in a way her condition made it harder for us, since now more than ever we had to shut up about anything she did that we mightn't like – it was absolutely crucial to keep her happy. And in the transition from trying to conceive, to her now being pregnant, it sometimes seemed as if we'd merely exchanged one set of problems for another. Every other day something seemed to crop up; we couldn't relax at all for fear of what new crisis lay round the corner.

A major worry was whether she'd look after her health – and by implication, the baby's. To my mind, as far as having your own baby's concerned, it's always difficult to believe that anyone else can do as good a job as you would yourself, and when I'd been pregnant I was mega-conscientious. I didn't smoke, I wouldn't even sniff alcohol, I ate all the right foods, I made sure I got plenty of gentle exercise. At the same time, we'd always felt that if we went into surrogacy we couldn't expect to dictate everything to the surrogate – however much we might want to. We couldn't tie her down or put her in a cage and say right, you stay there and you eat this and you will not smoke and you will not drink: that just wasn't on. She was a separate, different person, and we had to leave her to lead her own life, even if she held part of our life in her hands. All we could do was to keep our fingers crossed and try to guide and support her as much as we could to ensure she took care of herself.

But it wasn't easy. We'd all agreed it would be best if Stephanie avoided drinking and smoking, especially in the early stages of pregnancy when the foetus is most vulnerable. But in reality, there were a couple of occasions when I saw her drinking and having the odd cigarette, and even though I told her there and then I'd definitely rather she didn't smoke at least, I knew that no matter what I said, she could quite easily please herself after I was out of sight. Though she wasn't indulging heavily in either habit, and I'm sure she gave up cigarettes eventually, still, in those months it gave me a sick feeling to think that she was feeding this child on alcohol and smoke. I found it horrendous not to know what she was doing, and to have to wonder whether she really was looking after herself as much as she might if the baby were hers.

With such anxieties cropping up pretty regularly in my waking life, it's hardly surprising my sleep became fairly turbulent. With the advent of the pregnancy, my tormenting dream about Emma's birth ceased, but I started to have other troubling visions. Two weeks after we learnt Stephanie was pregnant, I dreamt *I* was in hospital, not Stephanie, with the baby – again a girl. I looked at the little thing and saw, to my dismay in the dream, that she had Stephanie's lips. 'Oh no,' I thought, but then she smiled up at me, and looked just like Mark – really cheeky. I cried with happiness, and then realized I didn't have anything for the baby – no clothes, no nappy, nothing. I had to ask a nurse to lend me things!

A little later I dreamt Mark and I had been away for a couple of days, when we suddenly remembered we hadn't fed the baby (yet again, she was a daughter). We ran and ran till we reached home, thinking she'd be dead, and found her, still alive, in her pram. Panicking, we raced to sterilize the bottles, with me screaming in frustration because I couldn't just breastfeed the baby quickly there and then to save time.

I guess these dreams reflected some of my anxieties about how we were going to cope with the baby when it actually arrived. Most of the time I wasn't aware of worrying about this side of things, the practical business of caring for the baby wasn't something that bothered me, but we did have a problem inasmuch as we would somehow have to explain to people how we'd magically had a baby without my showing any signs of being pregnant.

Originally I thought of several ways, none of them practical, and one or two of them downright silly. I thought that perhaps we could emigrate, but that really wasn't a possibility; and then I wondered whether I couldn't just put a couple of cushions inside my jersey for a few months when I went out, to satisfy the natural curiosity of acquaintances such as the man in the corner shop, who'd certainly be astonished to find me suddenly coming in with a brand-new baby, when in casual conversation in the past I'd told him we weren't planning to have children for the moment – not wanting to go into the whole story of my life.

Well, the cushions idea was crazy of course: supposing I'd then bumped into someone who knew I couldn't have children, what would they have thought – that I'd finally flipped, no doubt! No, we needed an answer that would do for anyone and everyone who might ask, so it was doubly hard. We deeply resented the fact we couldn't just tell the truth – after all, it *was* Mark's baby! – and had to behave as if we were somehow ashamed of what we were doing, which we weren't at all. But the fact of everything being cloak-and-dagger made it seem as if there was a stigma attached to it, when had it not been for the fear of what action the social services would take, we'd have made it crystal clear we felt the reverse – that surrogacy should be accepted, that people should know about it and understand from couples like ourselves why it was necessary to take such a step.

In the end we settled on a half-truth; we'd tell people we were adopting, which would be the case insofar as we would be applying to adopt as soon as seemed advisable. This story made it easier to account for all the baby equipment we were steadily accumulating as the months went by; but we soon found out that an amazing number of people seemed to be in the know about adopting and how difficult it was to adopt a small baby. Eventually, we decided that if people started to ask more informed questions, or were suspicious, we'd have to resort to lying, saying that it was a special needs baby, not handicapped, but with a less severe special need, such as epilepsy. It was an awful burden, having to live a lie; the only thing that made it tolerable was the fact Mark and I had each other and such a strong relationship we didn't hide anything from one another. Though we might be having to lie to other people, at least it was a problem we shared; we both had to use the same excuses, and go through the same anguish about doing that.

Meanwhile, a brighter aspect of my relationship with Stephanie at this time was the baby, and sharing with her in its development. I'll always be enormously grateful to her for suggesting that I participate in the pregnancy like this – I wouldn't have missed it for the world. I feel very privileged to have had that opportunity, and though Stephanie and I didn't have a deep, earth-mother type intimacy about it, the fact that I accompanied her to all her antenatal checks, scans and classes did gradually create a stronger relationship between us, and was also a constant reminder to all of us that the child she was carrying was to be Mark's and mine, not hers. I don't mean this in a harsh or hard-hearted way. But I do believe very strongly that in something as potentially volatile and emotional as pregnancy, where a woman may change, and inevitably becomes attached to the baby inside her, any surrogate mother needs as much support as she can get to help her keep the crucial detachment that will enable her to give the child to the couple at the end. For her part, Stephanie was always very strong-minded about this, and her attitude towards the baby was everything one could have wished for. She was very fond of it, but she always thought and talked of it as mine and Mark's.

'Your baby's kicking me,' she'd say. 'Come and calm her down for me, Rona.'

As often as not, when I laid my hand on her belly, the baby would quiet again, and I'd say triumphantly, 'See! She's going to be all right for me!'

Stephanie did all this quite naturally, without any trace of it seeming forced – something I found amazing, and really admired in her. Her attitude, and our close contact, also helped both Mark and me to form a bond with the baby before it was born; we started to feel for it as our own, and understand the reality of the fact we were shortly going to be parents.

Stephanie's first scan brought this home to me quite forcefully – having sight of the baby for the first time, knowing that there it was, a tiny, perfect person growing away in there. Stephanie herself was very excited, and immediately started asking what names we were going to choose. It was lovely to share in that moment.

I enjoyed it the more because it didn't upset me at all.

That may sound strange, but the night before, out of the blue, I'd suddenly had misgivings about going. I wrote in my diary:

> Had a bad night – couldn't sleep at all – thought about Emma and her scan and how I watched her little arm wave about – laughing that that was her badminton arm. When I look at that screen tomorrow will I see Emma's arm again? I'm very afraid of my reaction – hadn't thought about it before . . .

For alongside my joy at the new life that was coming, ran the same seam of grief for the child we had lost; the wound was as deep as ever, and as April turned to May and the anniversary of Emma's death drew nearer, a terrible sadness seeped from that scar, troubling me, blurring with tears my visions of the happiness to come. In the small hours of 14 May I wrote:

> 1 a.m. – been in bed for two-and-a-half hours and still can't sleep. There's too many things in my mind. I'm beginning to worry about how I will cope with the baby. I know I'll love her as my own, she's Mark's child, but more and more my thoughts are with Emma and all that could have been. I desperately want to get on – and most days I do – it's the nights which are so bad. Why we have to go through all this anxious trauma I'll never know but I hope to all that's right and good that we're doing the right thing. Dear Lord, help me to go the right way, I don't want to hurt anyone, or step on anyone's toes, I hate deceiving Rev. Swinton by not telling him the whole truth, I so dearly wanted to tell him from the beginning but I couldn't, I pray he can forgive me and see why I did what I did.

The grief was as inescapable as it had ever been, and with the time of Stephanie's pregnancy coinciding so closely with that of mine the year before (both babies being due in late October), inevitably there were some eerie echoes. I'd first felt Emma move on 19 May, the previous year; now, on 21 May we had a phone call from Richard telling us that Stephanie was in the shower and had just felt the baby kick for the first time. Of course we were thrilled; yet I couldn't help remembering that day when I'd lain in the sun with Emma stirring in my own womb, and the memory brought to mind the other, darker moments that had followed hard upon the heels of that joy.

Diary, 23 May 1989:

12 p.m. Feeling very depressed tonight. 28 May [the anniversary of Emma's death] is very near – I dearly wish we could go to church on that day but unfortunately it's the day we fly out to Crete. It's not right. I don't want to go that day – I'm so afraid I'll burst into tears on the plane, in the airport, I just want to be alone with Mark, to remember. He's the only one who can share this sadness. Should we look at the pictures of Emma – the hospital still have them – I want to see her – why couldn't I have held her to say goodbye properly – I know she would not have looked like we imagined but would it have mattered?

We did fly to Crete then: we wanted both to celebrate our first wedding anniversary with a second honeymoon, and to get away together from some of the strains of the situation at home, especially at this time of remembering. So 28 May found me in Greece, far from home, far from the hospital where I'd been this time the year before. But thoughts of Emma were closer than ever, clustering round, thronging my throat with tears. In my diary I wrote to her of my unspeakable love and grief.

Dear Emma,
Nothing else can happen on this day – it's your day and no one else's. I love you still my darling, but I wonder if the pain of your leaving will ever go. Every night I torment myself, why, why, why. Why did they take you. No matter what happens nothing will ever replace

you Emma, you'll always be inside me in spirit forever more.

That night, Mark and I talked at length about what had happened, and how I was or wasn't coping after a year. Mark said he was concerned that I was maybe feeling sorry for myself rather than the baby, and that though he knew we'd never forget her, he wondered whether I wasn't feeling these emotions negatively now, in a way that made things worse, made them drag on and on. I was already very distressed, and I completely misinterpreted what he meant, and became terribly, terribly upset. I felt I wasn't being allowed to have the feeling that I had; I cried out that I had a lot to feel sorry about, and anyway, that I couldn't help it, and yes, I wanted to help myself feel better, but I didn't know what to do to help myself.

'If I have these feelings,' I said, 'how can I force them to go away? They're there, and whether I'm feeling sorry for myself, or what, I don't know, but I don't really care. I just want you to understand, so I can grieve when these special feelings are with me. All I want is for you to have your shoulder there when I need you, and for us *both* to remember always and not be afraid to talk about Emma.'

Well, I'd misunderstood him absolutely. I thought he'd been saying this because he was getting fed up with my constant grieving, he thought I should be over it by now; whereas in fact he was trying to help, by seeing if we could acknowledge whether any of my feelings were purely negative, and if so, if we could somehow re-route them, turn them into positive ones. I had partly got so distraught because I wondered if he still felt as I did; Mark doesn't express his emotions openly, easily, and since the time in hospital, though *I* was often weeping at the memories, I'd never seen him cry. I wanted to know that I wasn't alone in my sadness; we'd shared everything so far, I couldn't bear it if now I had to face this on my own.

But I needn't have worried. Mark assured me, 'Please don't think that because I'm not crying now, I'm not grieving. I feel exactly the same as you, but I just can't show it all the time.

Also, I've felt you've been suffering so, I had to try and put a brave face on, to be strong . . .'

Once I understood this, the storm passed: and, as is the way with storms, it left the air much clearer between us.

One thing refused to blow over, however: every month I debated with myself, should we look at the photograph of Emma, or not? At length, knowing that the new baby was on the way and would soon be here, I felt I had to try and put the matter to rest, to lay that ghost. In July I made a definite decision. I asked my doctor to write to the hospital, saying I wanted to see the photograph that was in my notes.

A few weeks later, I received a letter from Professor Churchill. It said that while nowadays it is usually normal practice to take photographs of any child that is above twenty weeks' gestation when it dies, this was not done in my case, and this had been clearly recorded in my notes.

The morning I got that letter I just wanted to put my fist through the window. I was angry, I just couldn't believe they could have done this. I thought Why? Why is there no photograph? I collapsed on the bed crying, sobbing uncontrollably.

Eventually, I rang my doctor. He was very sympathetic, but said there was no point in my looking for something that wasn't there, and that he guessed that what had happened was that the staff had been so involved in saving my life at the time, the matter of taking the photograph had perhaps simply been overlooked. It was very sad, but there was nothing that could be done about it now. I said I could see that and *was* immensely grateful for them saving my life, but I needed to have something I could look at, something tangible I could take in my hands that would tell me about the time I was there; so I'd like to see my hospital notes.

At that, he became very defensive. He asked what the point of that would be, and said the hospital wouldn't be happy to show notes to a patient – not that anybody was trying to cover anything up.

Now, I'd never suggested they *were*, so of course, this phrase started another hare in my mind, I thought, 'Why

did he say that? Is there something we were never told?'
I didn't voice this to him, just argued for a while that it
would do me good to see my notes; but it was no use, it
was like banging my head against a brick wall. He suggested
I come in to see him and discuss it, because he knew it was
yet another terrible blow; here I'd finally made up my mind
I wanted to see the photo, and now the decision had been
snatched out of my hands.

I rang off. I think things went from bad to worse in my
mind then, I felt I simply had to see my notes, I had to know
what had happened. I'd hoped the decision to see the photo
would allay some of my anguish: instead, I found I was in
an even more desolate predicament, with no photo and no
reason why.

I thought long and hard about it, and decided in the end
that I couldn't handle any more trauma, and wouldn't press
for the notes. But this still left me with the terrible aching
need to know why I'd been assured I could see a photograph
when in fact none was available.

On a friend's suggestion, I arranged to see Rev. Swinton
and Sister Grant. Being the hospital chaplain, and organizer
of the remembrance services for dead babies, Rev. Swinton
had regular contact with the pathology department, and
would probably know, or could discover, if there were any
photographs there; my friend, who was a midwife, explained
– another fact I didn't know – that autopsies were routinely
performed on all babies who died, and sometimes Pathology
took a photograph at that point, though usually only if there
was an abnormality. Though obviously such pictures were
potentially very upsetting, I felt such an overwhelming urge
to see Emma, that for me any photo was better than none
at all.

I saw Rev. Swinton and Sister Grant a few weeks later. It
transpired that by the time the pathologist received Emma's
body, she was quite tightly curled up, and the pathologist
had decided after much thought that in the circumstances it
was better not to take a photograph, as to do so would have
necessitated trying to uncurl Emma, which, it was implied,
would have involved breaking bones. The pathologist had

113

felt that for me to be shown a picture taken in such a situation would have been too cruel, and more distressing than not seeing one at all. So there was no photo and, as Professor Churchill had indicated, the reasons for this were clearly cited in my notes: it was just extremely unfortunate that there had been no other communication between Pathology and the nurses who looked after me after the operation, so they had – understandably – assumed that the photo would be there in my notes, as was usual in such cases.

This news cut deep: and to this day, in spite of the healing time and events that have passed since we lost Emma, it still haunts me that I never have seen, and never will see her, I'll never know what she looked like now. It's as if we're grieving for a ghost, and this makes it harder to accept, to resolve. Yet that meeting with Rev. Swinton and Sister Grant helped me enormously. As well as giving me that much-needed explanation, they again assured me it was entirely normal for me to feel as I did, and that I should never try to 'pull myself together' or forget, or leave the past alone. I must talk, think, cry and daydream about it all for as long as I needed; they would always be at the end of a phone if I wanted to speak to them or ask any more questions. Truly they were a great source of comfort and strength, and I'm so grateful to them for supporting me through those tormented times.

I needed all the support I could get, for meanwhile, we received a letter from Stephanie that knocked us for six. A few days previously we'd been out to the site to see her and Richard. We'd been delighted to see that everything between them seemed to be fine and rosy in the garden, and Stephanie herself looked very well and happy.

Then, on 4 July, came this letter:

Dear Rona and Mark,
I am writing this . . . as it is often difficult to see you when I feel I need to talk. Unfortunately I have let my problems build up, and have kept silent in the hope that they might eventually go, however I am now at a very

crucial point where I feel I can't take any more, and have had enough.

The problems are . . . firstly, this must be the most boring and depressing time of my life . . . Six days a week I am stuck in this cardboard box, with only 1 TV set for pleasure. I see Richard for a few hours in the evening before he falls asleep. Then I face hours of being alone again. I only go out on a Friday usually, and that is for shopping . . . I cannot afford to go anywhere else unless transport is provided . . . We don't really have money for enjoyment . . . I am trying to save up so Richard can have a decent 21st birthday. It looks like this may not be possible . . .

All this would mean nothing to me, if I wasn't so miserable. I can honestly say that I have put myself in your shoes, I feel deeply for your situation, because of this I have kept quiet, which is completely out of character for me. This is just . . . to ask you to see my point of view, we are all guilty of overlooking certain things, and taking each other for granted . . . We know the hours Mark works, we know often you are both tired. I am *not* asking for extra money so I can go out and be frivolous. Money is irrelevant when I need to be happy. If I was happy, I would not mind being stuck in so much. Please see my point of view, I at least thought you and your family would in some ways substitute my own that I am missing a great deal.

I have been here a year, through no fault of anyone's, and so far I have hated 90% of it. I would like to look back on this time with pleasure, but I know I won't be able to. I would like to have a few days when I'm not here, in a shop, or in Margaret's [my mother's], because that's all I do. I still have months to go, I can't stay here if the next four months are like the last. I know if I am happier, everything will be easier for me in the end. To be happy I need a little company sometimes, then lack of money would mean nothing.

I judge people as I find them, but sometimes I feel I hardly know you. I want to be so busy and occupied that

I hardly notice the baby. Now it is all I think about. It controls my diet, my social life, and even my love life. I need to do things unrelated to this baby, so I don't get attached. This letter is not meant to anger or annoy anyone . . . Don't take it the wrong way, but . . . I need support . . . The only alternative that I can see now is that I return to my family, and just come back for the birth . . . I feel you may not want to give any more time and support than you are now and you may feel this is best. Concerning the birth . . . the agreement Rona and I made is absolutely fine, and I would not change this in any way, you have my word on that. It is just the months leading up to the birth that are so depressing I want to cry just thinking about them.

Maybe you both feel happy as it is now, in that case I can receive support from my family instead, after all you can't be expected to be a complete substitute family . . .

Please understand that my feelings in no way alter my decision to give you your child, but I would like to be happy at the same time . . . Please do not be offended by anything I have written, I'd phone up but often there is no answer and the curtains move around here when I go out . . .

Contact me if you feel I am completely out of order, we all have our points of view. Otherwise I'll arrange a move of some sort.

Love Stephanie

9
GREAT EXPECTATIONS

The letter dropped on us like a bombshell; we were shattered. Its sadness shocked us profoundly, especially as the last time we'd seen Stephanie we'd thought she was happy; this was suddenly like a cry in the dark, full of a suffering we hadn't even guessed at. We felt awful, horrendously guilty that she was having our baby and it was making her miserable, and especially that we hadn't seen just how bad the situation had become for her. Her words on the page articulated her feelings much more eloquently than when she normally spoke, and suddenly it was as if we started to see her predicament clearly for the first time – how lonely and isolated she must be, stuck out on the site with no friends (Richard was at work during the day), no family, no transport (neither she nor Richard drove), not a lot of money, and nothing specific to do except wait for the birth, all the while trying not to think of the baby and of having to give it up.

The two of us sat down and had a long, hard think. We realized we hadn't imagined ourselves into her situation nearly enough, and had been too impatient with her, too hard on her. Just as this time had come to seem, for us, like taking a year or so out of our normal, married life as a couple, so now we saw that for her too this was a time of limbo, she was taking this year out of her own life story – only she was doing so essentially for us, to give us the ultimate gift of a child. We'd always been aware, at root, that this made her a special person, but we'd thought of it as something she'd wanted to do and was happy with. So as the months had gone by perhaps we had indeed, as she suggested, started to take what she was doing a little for granted, in the sense that we just hadn't made enough allowances for how she was feeling.

It all seemed worse, because we also felt we *had* tried to make her happy, by visiting her at least once a fortnight, and more usually once a week, giving her little gifts, talking things over constantly, and so on. All this time we'd thought we'd been making a big effort – I suppose it especially seemed that way because at the start we hadn't intended to have much close contact at all. Now I felt that for all these strivings and sacrifices, I'd failed Stephanie in one crucial way: I hadn't really let myself go to her, emotionally, because of my original deep fear of what would happen if we became very close and then she kept the baby. But her letter made us aware that we'd been wrong to assume close contact was a mistake; because, whatever *we* might feel about it, for Stephanie, the better she knew us, the easier it would be for her to give us the baby at the end. And now we remembered all Gena had said about the problems surrogates face, and how vital it is to make every possible attempt to see they are happy, and if necessary, humour them through a time that invariably involves a lot of changes, both physical and emotional.

We had to face facts: no matter what we'd *tried* to do, it wasn't enough. Stephanie wasn't happy, and it was up to us to see that she was. We went out to visit her that evening, and told her how sorry we were about everything, and particularly that she'd felt she couldn't speak to us directly about it, but had had to write. Curiously, she seemed brighter already, and said oh, not to worry, she'd been having an off day, things weren't really that bad . . . Maybe just getting it all off her chest had helped. I suggested we go and look at flats nearer the centre of town, so that she and Richard wouldn't be so isolated, and over the next week we did check out a few, but in the end she decided it would be easier to stay put.

A couple of nights after getting the letter, I dreamt that Stephanie had kept the baby until she was about four years old, and then said we could have her. The news came as a complete surprise to me: somehow, I hadn't even known she'd *had* the baby, let alone that she'd been keeping the little girl all this time – though Mark and all Stephanie's family knew. In the dream I saw the child hauntingly clearly: she didn't look like anybody in particular, but just like herself, and she was wearing a little brown duffle coat, white tights and a pair of small red shoes; she had shoulder-length, mousy coloured hair, blue eyes, and a lovely pure white complexion.

Though at the time, I dismissed the dream as daft, I can see now it reflected all the worry brought on by discovering how Stephanie really felt, and especially the fact of simply not having known what was going on in her mind. It underlined how far apart we seemed to have drifted from her even as we thought we were getting to know her better.

But the letter, however shocking to us, did improve our relationship with Stephanie. For a start, Mark and I did our best to be more understanding and tolerant, and redoubled our efforts to spend time with her and Richard. And, as is often the way with these things, what at first was a conscious effort on our part gradually became, the more we saw of them, a much more spontaneous and genuine friendship, something we took pleasure in and enjoyed sharing.

I don't know for certain if it helped Stephanie, if she felt the difference; I very much hope so, because we really did want her to be happy, I'd have done anything for her not to suffer. At any rate, she did seem more cheerful as the summer wore on. I know a lot of this was due to her relationship with Richard, which really blossomed. He'd always been so supportive of her, even in the bad times, and he was so proud of what she was doing; as she told me herself, he was her backbone, he kept her going even when she felt like giving up. So, when they told us in August that they planned to marry in the New Year, and start their own family, we were delighted. We knew this would make a lot of difference to how Stephanie felt after giving up the baby; as she said, 'Now I have the future to look forward to, I can make plans rather than just having to face a future of nothing.'

She also told me that this relationship with him had changed her values, she felt now that emotional relationships really meant something, and this had helped her to understand us a bit better and see why we'd wanted to go through with this, given the way we felt about each other. And so, gradually, as we all grew in awareness and understanding, our feelings for one another deepened, and we became friends.

Meanwhile, as the magic date drew nearer, there were 101 things I had to do in preparation for the birth and subsequent adoption. There was a mammoth amount of organization involved: it was very fortunate I wasn't working at the time, because the preparations in themselves constituted a full-time job – something I hadn't anticipated. It was partly so time consuming because, with surrogacy being such a taboo subject, there were no guidelines for us to follow, so it was a case of DIY from the outset.

Just finding out all the information about the different aspects, and trying to keep it all together in my mind, was horrendous; and of course, because we didn't know what would actually happen regarding social services and the adoption, we were trying to plan for every single little thing that could go wrong, which was a nightmare. Sometimes I got so tired of it all, I felt it was never-ending. It was as if my whole life was being swallowed up in this maze, there was no time to live our own lives together. We seemed to be in limbo twenty-four hours a day, wondering what could happen. The only way out seemed to be to take each day at a time, and remember, always, that we were going to have a baby.

During these months I turned constantly to Gena, who was a tremendous support and an absolute mine of information; and I also plundered other sources, such as the British Association for Adoption and Fostering (BAAF), the Scottish Adoption Service and the Adoption Counselling Service, regarding our adoption prospects and preparations. In July, I took our friend Susan's advice, and went through our whole case with a solicitor. It transpired that there was little we could do for the moment; most of the legal activity could only start once the baby was born. However, in the meantime, the solicitor said she would check out all the details as far as she could, so that when the time came, we'd be in a position to act at once.

At around the same time, I also contacted a social worker called Charles Sparrow, whom Gena had advised me was sympathetic to surrogacy. My main concern was whether he thought we should have what's called a 'home study' carried out in advance of the birth, to strengthen our case with the social services. Usually, in adoption cases, social services perform such a study on the prospective parents' home, to ensure that it's a suitable environment for the child. Gena had suggested that if we had a home study done by an independent social worker before the birth, then, if the social services tried to make the child a ward-of-court, we could produce the study as evidence that might forestall or reassure the authorities.

In the event, having heard our story, Charles said he didn't think this would be necessary, and as our solicitor was also of this opinion, we didn't have the study done. Charles agreed with the solicitor that because we wouldn't have been married two years by the time we had the baby, it was likely we'd have to endure an interim period of one year before our application to adopt it was finally approved, but he was very reassuring. He confirmed, as Gena and the solicitor had already said, that as long as Stephanie willingly gave up the baby, it would be very difficult for anyone to take it from us unless it could be proved we were negligent: in the case of a baby, as with anything else, possession is nine-tenths of the law. The main aim for us now was to make sure we got the baby safely into our home.

On the domestic front, there were dozens of practical preparations to see to. Firstly, as well as reading up everything I could about being a birth partner, and going with Stephanie to her antenatal classes, I was actually starting to prepare my own body for the birth – for I'd decided to try and breastfeed the baby if I possibly could. I knew this was better and more pleasurable for the baby, and I'd always wanted to breastfeed my own child; I also felt that if I could do it, it would help to form a very strong bond between me and the baby. I'd discovered from Gena and various other sources,

121

such as the La Lèche League (a society for the promotion of breastfeeding), that it was possible for adoptive mothers to do this using a combination of drugs and/or breast stimulation to build up a milk supply and trigger the 'let-down' reflex, which releases the milk. So, having ascertained from my doctor that I could speak to him in complete confidence, I told him that we were expecting a surrogate baby in the near future, and that I wanted to breastfeed, and asked him if he could prescribe the appropriate medication to help me. When he'd recovered from his astonishment, he readily agreed, and a few weeks before the baby was due I started to take a short course of a drug called Motillium.

Meanwhile, in July, I hired an electric breast pump from the National Childbirth Trust (NCT), in order to try and build up milk-producing tissue in my breasts. The pump basically worked by simulating the action of a suckling infant. I'd plug the machine into the mains, pop the suction cup on to one of my breasts, and sit while the pump sucked away. I had to do this for about twenty minutes each side, repeating the process every four hours. Neither my mother nor Stephanie much fancied the look of this to start with, but after the initial weirdness, I soon got used to it, and, ignoring the rude and ribald comments from various quarters, carried on regardless. Stephanie came round to the contraption eventually, and suggested she could try to use it in the hospital after the birth, to express colostrum and breastmilk for the baby's first few days. We wanted to give the baby the best possible start in life, but both felt it was better to avoid Stephanie actually putting the child to her breast, as this might create a bond between them she'd find impossible to break when it came to giving up the baby.

Aside from these biological concerns, I was busily amassing a mountain of things for the baby – my 'little empire', as Mark called it – and spending a fortune at Mothercare. Though the doctors who'd checked Stephanie were slightly worried that the baby seemed on the small side – Stephanie didn't appear to be gaining much weight – still, repeated scans and tracings on the hospital monitor showed that nonetheless it appeared to be perfect and moving about quite healthily. So, as the pregnancy ripened, I'd thrown caution to the wind and bought what could modestly be described as the full layette. I couldn't help myself. I took to going into the freshly decorated nursery and checking the inventory over and over: top-and-tail bowl, nappies, baby bath, swinging crib, and clothes, clothes, clothes galore. I'd go in every day and take it all out and look at it again; I tried on the baby carrier to see how it would fit and feel, and hugged the baby nest, and pushed the pram about with a doll in it. One evening Mark came in from work to find me sat on the floor there absolutely starry-eyed, with all the tiny bits and pieces scattered round me, dreaming away, in another world. He said I looked so secure and happy, it was as if I were building my nest, and gathering a hoard of small treasures with which to feather it.

I could hardly believe it was really going to happen; as the weeks went steadily by, my excitement rose up and up, and I started to wish the time away, longing for Stephanie to go into labour. Yet at the same time, as everything came to a head, I felt anxious. Only now, now that our life was about to change forever, did I start to wonder: had we done the right thing? How would I cope with the birth? What if something went wrong, now, at the last, after all the waiting? Sometimes, as I knelt in the nursery, thinking of the newborn baby I would soon hold here in my arms, cross-currents of such joy and fear swept through me, I could feel the tears starting to my eyes. I so badly wanted everything to turn out fine, the suspense was almost unbearable. 'Calm down,' I told myself, 'Stephanie's thirty-two weeks' pregnant now; we've come this far, nothing's going to go wrong.'

At the beginning of September, Stephanie and Richard went away for a fortnight's holiday, to another caravan about sixty miles away, near Lossiemouth. They'd been gone four days when, at one-thirty in the morning of 6 September, we got a phone call. I answered it.

Stephanie's voice said, very, very calmly, 'Rona, hello, I'm very sorry to bother you, I know it's late, but I'm bleeding, quite heavily, what shall I do?'

I said, 'OhmyGod!' and thought immediately 'Miscarriage'. I swallowed hard and went on, 'How bad is the bleeding? Have you any pains?'

'Well, it's like the start of a period, I've a few cramps, but we'd just had sex when it started, so . . .'

As soon as she said 'cramps' something in my stomach lurched, a horrible feeling which drained right down to my feet. But I had to be practical, at all costs I had to keep my wits about me, so I said, 'Right. Phone the nearest hospital, ask for the labour ward, tell them exactly what's happened, see what they say. Then let us know what's going on.'

Half an hour later she rang back. The message was garbled, but the gist of it was the staff had said she could go into hospital to be checked over just in case, but they didn't seem to think it was likely to be a serious problem. Stephanie herself said the bleeding had subsided a bit, and I could tell she wasn't keen to go into hospital. She suggested waiting an hour to see how things went.

I asked her, 'Stephanie, what does your gut feeling tell you is wrong?'

'My instinct says nothing's wrong, I'm fine, there's nothing to worry about, and if this was my baby I'd just get back into bed and rest. But this is *your* baby, Rona, I want you to say what you'd do in the circumstances.'

I was very touched that she said this, and didn't hesitate to reply, 'Get in a taxi and go to hospital, please!'

About an hour later we had a call from Richard. They were at the nearest hospital to Lossiemouth, Stephanie had been checked over by a midwife, and they'd decided to send her in an ambulance down to Aberdeen, to the hospital where she was booked to have the baby. Richard said it wasn't yet clear if there was a problem, but the staff thought Stephanie's own hospital had better run all the tests and scans to be on the safe side.

For the next couple of hours, Mark and I paced the flat. I felt cold, cold at the thought of what might be happening. It was horrible to know that Stephanie might actually be having the baby prematurely, or worse, that something else might have gone wrong, and yet to be in a position where everything was out of our control, there was nothing we could do but wait. All our hopes, our carefully laid plans, seemed to have been wiped out by one phone call.

The phone rang again.

'It's okay, everything's fine,' Richard said. 'We've arrived, we're in the hospital here, Stephanie's had all the tests, they've done a scan and monitored the baby, it's absolutely fine, there's nothing to worry about.'

He added that they'd thought at one point the bleeding might have indicated the placenta was lying low down in the uterus, which can be very dangerous and would have meant Stephanie would probably have had to stay in until the baby was born. But now they thought it wasn't that, but something called erosion of the cervix, which in spite of its gruesome name, apparently wasn't serious. They were going to keep her in for a day or so just to be sure.

The relief, the relief!

But I still couldn't relax completely until I'd seen her. I wanted to go to her there and then, and, as soon as time had passed and the hour was slightly more respectable, I called the labour ward, where she was, and enquired after her. The nurse on the line was very suspicious, but at last relented. 'She's fine, but you can't speak to her now, she's sleeping, and visiting hours aren't until seven o'clock this evening.'

At seven prompt Mark and I were at the hospital, flowers in hand. I was so looking forward to seeing Stephanie I could think of nothing else, so it was only as we made our way towards the west wing, where they'd told us she was, that I began to remember. Slowly but surely, inescapably, smells and sounds around me brought it all back. This was where *I* had been, last year. A feeling of dread gripped me, I started to hang back; without knowing it, I set off down the wrong corridor, and had to be called back by Mark; I blundered into a trolley, hardly aware of what I was doing, knowing only that it was here, here, that it had all happened.

When we finally got into the ward, I discovered that Stephanie's bed was right next to the little room where I'd been when I was in labour, losing Emma. As we passed, I looked in: there was another girl in there, and my heart went out to her, I wondered what she was going through. Then we were at Stephanie's bedside, and there she was sitting up, very calm and collected, cheerfully doing the crossword, eating chocolates, and bullying Richard as usual.

As we sat with her, my panic passed, the icy terror ebbed away. This was a different time, a different woman, a different pregnancy. It was going to be all right. Stephanie was covertly showing us a photo of the latest scan: we pounced on it excitedly, but though Mark immediately made sense of the fuzzy image, and could see the face quite clearly, I couldn't make head nor tail of it, and had to have it explained to me over and over before at last I picked out the baby's features. That was one good thing to come out of the whole scare: we felt reassured to know the child was well. Another positive aspect was that we made sure we really were ready for the birth – bag packed, house spick and span, breathing techniques learnt inside out.

But we also felt, now, we would have to put our reserve plan into action. From early in the pregnancy, we'd been wondering whether it mightn't be best to try and move to another town for the last couple of weeks and the birth itself, because of the fear that someone in the west wing of the labour ward would recognize either me or Mark. Mine had been such an unusual case, and I'd been in hospital for ten days, every shift on the ward at the time knew who I was; if anyone should remember me or Mark, and see us with a heavily pregnant woman, it seemed likely they'd put two and two together. And now, though nobody in fact remembered us on this visit to Stephanie, I had 'bad vibes' about being back in that place. There was a further complication. When this scare of Stephanie's had first happened, I'd told Richard to pass himself off at the hospital as her brother – but in the heat of the moment, Stephanie had said he was her boyfriend, and of course the staff had assumed he was the baby's father. This meant our plan for Mark to be declared the father at the birth, enabling him to spend as much time as he liked with the baby, might well be all to pot if Stephanie delivered here; as we were so near her due date, it was quite possible that when she went into labour, someone would recognize one or other of us from this incident, and remember that on her earlier visit it was Richard who was supposed to be the father.

Actually being in that labour ward, and so near to 'D-Day', brought home forcibly the reality of our situation. We couldn't take any more chances. Mercifully, we *hadn't* lost this baby through miscarriage; we certainly weren't now going to have it whisked away from us by the social services through someone at the hospital rumbling us. We'd have to go elsewhere, and soon.

So in the weeks immediately after Stephanie came out of hospital, I had yet another thing to arrange: finding temporary accommodation for me, Stephanie and Richard in Dundee. Mark wouldn't be able to accompany us; he was saving all his leave for the time of the birth, and anyway someone had to hold the fort at home, look after the dog and keep up appearances with the neighbours.

We decided to move as late as possible into the pregnancy, so we wouldn't be stuck in a strange place for weeks and weeks, just waiting for the big event, and also because it was best for Stephanie to have as much continuity of antenatal care as possible, rather than having to change hospitals a while before her due date. After much searching and scouting round, I managed to book a holiday cottage for three or provisionally four weeks from 21 October. This would give us a week before Stephanie was due, and allowed for the baby being late (though Stephanie was convinced it was going to be a week early!); it also permitted us to stay on in the cottage for the ten days after the birth. We wanted to stay there for that period because we'd decided it would be best for us to remain all together for the days when the midwife had to visit. That way, from the point of view of the social services, there wouldn't be anything suspicious going on. The set-up would be just the same as for the birth: Stephanie, obviously, was the baby's mother; Mark would pass for Stephanie's boyfriend, and so could act naturally as the child's father; I would be her best friend and birth partner; and Richard would pass for her brother.

Unfortunately, this meant he wouldn't be able to be there at the birth, which would be very tough on him emotionally – but there was no way round this if Mark was to have the chance to see his child born and have unlimited access to it after the birth. Naturally, there'd be restrictions on who could or could not be there when Stephanie was in labour, and on visiting afterwards. So, after some discussion, we'd decided that if only one person was allowed in for the birth, it would be me, since Mark as the baby's father would be allowed to stay much longer once the child was born, whereas, as a 'friend', I wouldn't get as much opportunity to see and hold the baby unrestrainedly.

There were a couple more hurdles to get over before we could leave for the cottage. Stephanie had to tell the hospital she was likely to be moving just before the birth, and ask if she could have her antenatal notes to pass on to the next hospital where she'd be having the baby. We'd agreed she should be fairly vague about the time of the move, to prevent anyone from tracking her down there or trying to stop her going. But in the event, they made no fuss about it at all, and handed over the notes without a murmur.

Secondly, the day before we left, I finally told my father (who is separated from my mother) the truth about the situation. We'd said all along we were adopting a special needs baby, because I'd been very worried about his reaction to surrogacy. However, now we were so close to the birth, I felt I had to come clean. To my amazement, he knew a lot about surrogacy, he'd read about Gena's case when it happened, and he was very sympathetic and supportive. He admitted he'd been very worried about us having a special needs child, and the strain this might have put on our lives. He wished us very well in this, and said he'd be looking forward to seeing the baby as soon as we got home.

With these good omens, I should have been feeling pretty cheery on the eve of the move. But I was dreading leaving Mark for what seemed like such a long time – and worse, we didn't even know just how long it might be. I was determined to come back for flying visits now and again, but still, the prospect of separation seemed grim, especially at such an emotionally stressful time, when we most needed to be together. Somehow, in all the preparations and anxieties, the fact of the birth had been slightly overshadowed recently: but now, with only a week left to the due date, it was as if we'd suddenly come down to earth and remembered, 'Hang on a minute, by this time next week we could have this tiny baby!' It was a weird feeling. From our point of view, though we'd done everything we should, and thought of little else, we hadn't been intimately involved, minute by minute, in the physical fact of the pregnancy. I'd seen all the scans, yes, and we'd felt the baby moving, but it wasn't like living day-to-day through your own pregnancy and sharing with your husband in that growing process. Outwardly, we had nothing physically to show we were having a baby – yet at any moment now, we might bring that baby home. It was as if there was a link missing in the chain.

Also, the nearer we got to the due date, the more scared I became. This was something we'd fought for, we'd strived to reach this point, and as the moment drew nearer I was more and more worried about what was going to happen. I wasn't anxious about Stephanie giving us the baby; I knew she would, I had that much trust and faith in her. No, my nerves were more about the time *after* the birth, I foresaw horrendous problems with the social services.

At the same time, I longed for the waiting to be over. Though outwardly, so much had happened in the past year, inside, life for me had just been a case of going through the motions of day-to-day living. As far as I was concerned, once the baby was born, my life was going to start. I felt that everything that had occurred since we came off the plane after our honeymoon just shouldn't have happened; we'd had so many problems to deal with, we hadn't really had a life. It was as if we were climbing a hill, and only when the baby was born would we reach the top and start our married life together.

But for the moment we'd have to be apart. On 21 October, Stephanie, Richard and I moved to the cottage. The move went fine, though to begin with I felt terrible about it. By the second night I was dreadfully homesick – it was the first night for ages I'd slept alone – and felt empty and lonely and lost. Stephanie and Richard had gone to bed and were watching TV in their room; I sat alone in mine, listening to the wind and wishing the weeks away. The cottage was in a small town a few miles from the city – it was a stagnant no-man's-land, the sort of place where the kids got their fun by screaming round on motorbikes. I could hardly bear to think we might have to be there for another four weeks – it seemed like an eternity.

Things improved after a few days, however. Now we were actually living together, I got to know Stephanie and Richard much better, and they were very good company. Stephanie particularly always kept me amused, and as the week passed by and her due date drew nigh, we started to confide in each other and became very close. She was so spirited and determined, so calm and sensible, that it was impossible not to admire her.

I asked her how she felt about the baby; she told me she was very fond and proud of it, but didn't feel she had a maternal bond with it; she thought of it more as a little friend she was caring for just for a while. I believed her: she spoke so naturally and honestly, there was nothing forced about her words. Incredibly, wonderfully, she'd managed to nurture this baby for nine months and yet maintain enough distance from her own flesh to hold fast to her resolve. Now all we had to do was make sure she and the baby came safely through the birth.

In the first week at the cottage, we went together to the hospital so Stephanie could be checked over and see where she'd be having the baby. It seemed a nice enough place, though we were a bit disconcerted when the staff said they wanted to give Stephanie yet another scan – about the seventh she'd had during the pregnancy – and run a trace on the baby's movements, because they wanted to check it for size. When we got up to the scan department, they refused to let me go in with Stephanie; apparently, if I'd wanted to accompany her, we should have booked ourselves a 'social scan'. I was so furious, I was tempted to ask whether this meant we should take in a bottle of gin or something . . . However, it went fine, and the baby registered ten out of ten on the trace for movements, so all was well. We came away reassured – if nonetheless impatient.

The twenty-ninth of October came; but the baby didn't. It was hard to cope with the sense of anticlimax; we seemed now to have stepped over into limboland, living on borrowed time. We tried to while away the hours by going out and taking lots of photographs. The one consolation of the grim town was its position right by the sea; we could walk along the shore and watch the waves roll in, repeating themselves over and over in a slow sure tide of renewal.

Three long days later, we went with Stephanie for her routine antenatal check at the hospital. As usual, she submitted a urine sample, and as usual, she was examined and her blood pressure taken.

Then the doctor sat down with us and said quietly, 'Well, the baby seems fine, it's moving about well, but you've got two counts of protein in your urine, and your blood pressure's rather high, so it may be you're suffering from pre-eclampsia, and just to be on the safe side I'd like you to come into hospital today for twenty-four hours' observation.'

I really didn't take in what he'd said, I'd just been sitting there smiling and nodding all through this little speech, so his last few words sent me into shock. A sick feeling passed right through me. Luckily, Stephanie still had her wits about her, and asked quite calmly what pre-eclampsia was and what it would mean. The doctor replied that it occurred quite commonly in late pregnancy, and wasn't necessarily serious at this stage. But if left unattended, it could develop into eclampsia, which could cause the mother to have fits, and might damage the baby, so it was important to keep tabs on it early on, to stop it getting that far. They would admit Stephanie into hospital that evening and keep her in for twenty-four hours, during which time her blood pressure and urine would be checked at four-hourly intervals. If the condition worsened, they'd probably have

131

to induce the labour in order to save the baby. Though this wouldn't be too serious from the child's point of view – as Stephanie was already past her due date – we both knew that induction might well make labour more painful and unpleasant for her.

I must say I panicked a bit, but Stephanie stayed calm and collected even as we arrived back at the cottage and started to get everything ready for her going in. I still felt sick, terrified that at the last minute something was going badly wrong. The last thing I wanted was to have to leave Stephanie in hospital on her own when she was forty weeks' pregnant and might be induced at any moment. I felt powerless, as if everything were slipping through my fingers. There seemed to be nothing I could do to help.

At around six o'clock, we took Stephanie back into hospital to be admitted. She was examined again, and her blood pressure taken twice more. Before she got into bed for the night the doctor told us it looked as if things weren't as bad as he'd initially thought. Her blood pressure had gone down again, and there was a possibility she might just have a urine infection, but they'd keep her in till the following afternoon to be sure.

There was nothing more for Richard and I to do but try to disguise our relief and leave Stephanie to get some sleep. I phoned the hospital later that night, and again first thing in the morning, to see how she was. Each time, I held my breath; and each time, the news was good. Her condition was stable, all was well. She was discharged from hospital on the afternoon of 2 November.

On the evening of the fourth, a Saturday, I left Richard and Stephanie – perfectly well, and still pristinely pregnant – at the cottage and drove home to spend that night and the Sunday with Mark. I was relieved at how well Stephanie seemed, and felt I could look forward to my brief trip home without having to worry. I hadn't seen Mark for a week, and it was lovely to be home again, however fleetingly: I would return to the cottage the following evening.

Any plans we were harbouring for a romantic Sunday

morning lie-in were soon blown out the window. At nine o'clock sharp we were woken by the urgent cry of the telephone, insistently demanding immediate attention. Reluctantly, I dragged myself out of bed and answered.

It was Richard. Stephanie had been experiencing period-type pains for some hours now and, though she wasn't sure, she thought she was in labour.

10
THE BIRTH

When I reached the cottage at around ten-thirty that morning, I found Stephanie was up and walking about to try and ease the pain. She looked perfectly composed, though rather pale and tired; she'd been awake since about half-past six, unable to sleep for the cramps. These were now coming every ten or even five minutes, but she said she couldn't tell whether they were 'proper' contractions or not, though the pain was quite bad. It was hard to know what was best to do. We'd agreed beforehand it would be wise to stay at the cottage until she was well into labour, to save having to wait for hours in hospital; as yet, Stephanie said she hadn't had a show, and her waters hadn't broken, so it seemed that if this *was* labour, it could only be the very start.

However, we decided to ring the hospital anyway, to see what they thought. Richard went off to the nearest phone box – there was no phone in the cottage – while I stayed with Stephanie and tried to help by chatting to take her mind off the pain. When Richard returned, he said the hospital had suggested staying put, because they didn't think Stephanie's 'symptoms' sounded like the onset of established labour; but Richard had insisted that we'd better go in. It was only a couple of days since Stephanie had been discharged from hospital following the pre-eclampsia scare, and he felt that even if she wasn't in labour now it would be best to find out just what was going on.

When we got to the hospital, Stephanie was put on a bed and a monitor fastened round her tummy to check on the baby's heart and the strength of the contractions. The baby seemed fine, but the staff said there wasn't much point in examining Stephanie internally at this stage, since the monitor had shown the contractions were only very mild, so there was a long way to go yet.

By the time they'd removed the monitor, it was around twelve-thirty, and though I'd told Mark when I left that I wouldn't call him until Stephanie had been examined, I now thought I'd better let him know what was happening. So I trotted off to the phone and told him there was no hurry, it wasn't worth him setting off just now, as it looked as if we'd be in for quite a wait before things really got under way. In fact the nurses had said it could just be a false alarm.

When I got back to the first-stage labour room where Stephanie was, she was about to be given some lunch. She said the pain seemed to be getting worse, so I massaged her back, and got a bean-bag out for her to try and find a more comfy position. I stayed while she ate her food, chatting about this and that, and wondering whether this really was labour or not – even the nurses didn't seem convinced. At round about quarter to three, I said I thought I'd better go and find Richard, who'd had to wait in the corridor all this time, and go and grab some lunch myself, as I was absolutely famished and we could be there for hours. Stephanie seemed reasonably comfortable, so I said I'd be back as soon as possible and left her to it.

Richard and I returned from the canteen within half an hour. As we were making our way back to Stephanie's room, a nurse waved me down and asked, 'Are you the girl who's here as Stephanie Cottam's birth partner?'

'That's right, yes.'

'Well, you'd better hurry along. She's in delivery room one, and she's about halfway there.'

'*What?*'

'Yes, they've taken her to the delivery room.'

I couldn't believe it! In thirty minutes, Stephanie had gone from maybe not being in labour at all – according to the staff – to being halfway to giving birth. Though my mind was fixed on getting to her side as soon as possible, I just managed to ask, 'Have I time to ring her 'boyfriend' [Mark, in other words] and tell him what's going on?'

'Okay, yes, but you'd better be quick.'

135

Leaving poor Richard to wrestle with his worries in the waiting room, I rushed off to the phone.

'Mark? She's in labour, they've taken her into delivery room one, she's about halfway there, get here *now*!'

'I'm on my way.'

I ran back down the corridor and into the delivery room, expecting to find that Stephanie would have just arrived and be getting ready, but no, to my dismay, she was already fully cloaked out in a hospital gown, up on the bed, gas mask on . . . *In Labour.*

As I caught sight of her my heart turned over, I felt so guilty at having left her in such a vulnerable state. I dashed to her and gave her a great big hug and a kiss, and she took my hand and squeezed it really tightly.

I said, 'God, Stephanie, I'm really sorry, I thought I'd plenty of time, I've only been away half-an-hour . . . How on earth did this happen?'

In between gulps of gas and air, she managed to say, 'I've only just come in, it all happened really quickly . . . I was five centimetres dilated by the time the doctor examined me . . .'

From then on, it was all go. I took my shoes and jumper off – it was very warm in the room – and started to try and help Stephanie breathe slowly, deeply and rhythmically, which was a little difficult, as she wouldn't let go of the gas mask. I saw she was lying flat on her back, even though she'd originally said she wanted to use the birth chair and sit in a vertical position, as we'd read that this would make her less liable to tear, and she was anxious to avoid an episiotomy if at all possible. Though there were two midwives in with us, neither of them seemed to be doing much to help Stephanie get more comfortable. So I asked her if she wouldn't rather use the chair, or at least sit up, but she shook her head and said she didn't want to move now. Then she squeezed my hand tight, tight. I put my arm round her shoulder, and kept her hair back while I mopped her brow. I asked her if she'd like me to massage her back, but she said no, she was all right for the moment as she was, all she wanted was to keep a vice-like grip on my hand.

For the next hour or so it seemed that all I could do was to hold her hand, and help her pace her breathing more evenly. It was very erratic by now, and she was hanging on to the gas and air for grim death. It was a terribly helpless situation: I was so upset that I'd missed her being brought into the delivery room, she'd had to go through that alone, and now all I wanted was for everything to go fine for her, for her to have the best she could possibly have – I suppose, for her to go through it and have no pain. I'd have done anything to take the pain away. If only I could have gone through that labour for her! I could hardly bear to see her suffer – and all so that Mark and I might have our baby. I felt we'd put her in this situation, and now there seemed almost nothing I could do to help. As I held her, I guessed from the grip of her hand on mine how the pain racked and wrung her; I felt as if she were my sister and I *must* somehow spare her this suffering.

If I couldn't actually take the pain away, I was going to make damn sure she had everything she wanted – and none of the things she didn't. She'd said she wouldn't have an epidural unless it was absolutely essential, she'd try to get through on just the gas and air and Pethidine. By this time, they'd given her one shot of Pethidine, and said it could take about half an hour to take hold; but half an hour passed, and Stephanie's pain seemed to be no better. She was basically getting through her labour on nothing but gas and air and sheer determination. My admiration for her deepened by the minute.

I felt fiercely protective of her now, and maybe this coloured my view, but it seemed to me the midwives really weren't helping her much. At one point, a midwife from the local clinic came in, took one look at us both there on the bed, and couldn't resist adding her words of wisdom.

'Now look, Stephanie dear, you've got no rhythm, you've got to take slow, deep breaths in, then blow out again, slowly and deeply, slowly and deeply . . .' – all this said with her face right up close to Stephanie's; I'm sure she meant to help, but if I'd been in Stephanie's position, I doubt whether the words 'You've got no rhythm' directed within two inches of my nose would have made me feel on top of the world.

The midwife then turned her attention to taking me in hand: 'Look now, Rona, you know you could be here for long enough, this has only just started, you could be in for a long night ahead, so don't let Stephanie squeeze your hand in that position. Leave your hand flat, so she can't really hurt you. And look, you've got your arm round her shoulder! You're going to be sore if you're like this for hours and hours on end, you'll be in agony tomorrow! Try and get into a more comfortable position dear, and don't let her hurt you . . .'

Again, I'm sure she meant well, but I just couldn't believe she was saying this – there was poor Stephanie going through all this pain, and the midwife seemed most worried about *me*, and the way I was sitting! I didn't care a damn if I was sore in the morning, or my shoulder dropped off, or Stephanie crushed my hand to pulp; as long as my holding her, and her holding me, helped her, that was all I cared about.

As soon as the midwife had gone I said to Stephanie, 'To pot with that! You squeeze my hand if you want, take no notice of her, Stephanie.'

At about four o'clock, Stephanie started to feel the urge to push. One of the midwives asked her if she could come off the gas and air now, she'd need to be free of it in order to push the baby out properly; but Stephanie just refused to relinquish the mask, she clung to it like a limpet. Seeing her desperation, the midwife said nothing more for the present, but I could tell she didn't hold out much hope that Stephanie would be able to push effectively while filled with enough gas to launch a hot-air balloon. And indeed the poor lass did look pretty zombified by now; she was as droopy-eyed as a basset hound, her head was limp and her body all floppy; as I told her at the time, she looked as if she'd had about fifty vodkas. This rag-doll state would have been fine if it had been a sign of true relaxation, but I could tell she was still fighting the pain, for at the height of every contraction her shoulders would tense and rise up, in spite of my efforts to help by reminding her to push them down and relax every part of her body including her hands and feet. Still, she managed to joke along with me through parts of the labour; she might be battered in body, but her sense of humour remained grittily intact.

The head midwife now instructed Stephanie to listen carefully to the student midwife, Debbie, who was going to deliver the baby. 'Just listen to Debbie, nobody else will speak to you' – a fairly broad hint to me to shut up, I reckoned – 'She's going to tell you what to do, you must try and concentrate on what she's saying and do exactly what she tells you.'

Though I was loath to let go of Stephanie, I also didn't want to irritate the midwives by getting in the way, so I stepped back a couple of paces and sat down on the seat they'd placed by the bed for me.

Debbie then said to Stephanie, 'Right now, as soon as you feel a contraction starting, I want you to put your chin on your chest, take a deep breath, hold it, and push down in your bottom, push down there as you have the contraction.'

For the first couple of contractions, she'd say 'Push now' once, apparently hoping Stephanie was taking this in while at the height of a contraction and gasping on the gas and air. By this time, about half-a-dozen tiny hairs could be glimpsed emerging down below; I was totally flabbergasted, I just couldn't believe it, and jumped off my seat and cried, 'Stephanie, Stephanie! You can see the hair, you can see the hair, the head's almost there!'

I was beside myself with excitement – Stephanie had only been in there for just over an hour, and already the baby was nearly born – and I really wanted to egg her on, but felt I couldn't actually start advising her to push with the midwives standing there. I didn't want to interfere, but at the same time, I wasn't going to let them take over completely, and I could see that either Stephanie couldn't hear what Debbie was saying, or she wasn't listening, she was so far gone with the gas, for she wasn't responding to the midwife's instructions.

The head midwife stepped in. 'Now Stephanie, you're going to have to give up the gas and air, you've got to push this baby out, she's waiting there, she's just dying to come out.'

I couldn't resist trying to persuade Stephanie in my own way. 'Come on Stephanie, you said I could have a whiff of that gas and air, so let me have a go, give me that mask now . . .'

But it was no use. The way she hung on to the mask you'd have thought it was part of her own hand we were trying to take away.

The head midwife turned to me then and said, 'Well Rona, if you want to go and sit her up a bit more and stay there with her for support, we don't mind that, it'll help her get her chin to her chest better . . .'

Without more ado, I dived in again. I don't know whether I did the right thing or not, but I started to repeat everything Debbie said to Stephanie, for it seemed to me the midwife had lost all faith in her and didn't speak with much conviction. Her heart just wasn't in it, and anyway I was much more in tune with Stephanie than she was. I repeated Debbie's instructions, but about a hundred times more forcefully, urging Stephanie on, trying to show her with every syllable that I knew she could do it, that she was amazing.

I didn't have to pretend, either, for I was absolutely astonished as I watched the baby's head inching forward push by push, before dropping back again into the birth canal each time. It was the most incredible sight, to see our baby making its slow progress out into the world, the face still tantalizingly hidden, but showing a little more at every push.

My amazement soon turned to consternation, however, when after what could only have been about ten pushes at the most, the head midwife said to Stephanie – again at the height of a contraction, hardly the best time to speak to her – 'Look now, Stephanie, I think we're going to have to give you an episiotomy [cutting the skin between the vagina and the anus to speed up the delivery]. Do you understand what this involves?'

Stephanie, still in the throes of the contraction, couldn't speak, but I could see she was struggling to ask 'Why?'

— we'd both dreaded this eventuality. It had been agreed beforehand that if she couldn't speak for herself, I would speak for her, and the staff were to answer me, so I quickly said, 'Why does she have to have this? She doesn't want it, does she *need* to have this? Is she going to tear?'

Debbie said 'No, it's not that she's going to tear, it's because the baby's so tired now, we can see from the monitor that it's very weak and in a bit of distress, we've got to get it out as quickly as possible, and I'm afraid Stephanie just hasn't got the strength to push as hard as she needs to. She's taken so much gas and air, she thinks she's pushing really hard, but she's not able to make as strong an effort as she could have done if she'd had less gas and air. If we do the episiotomy, we can get the baby out more quickly, without Stephanie having to push much harder for longer.'

I must have looked doubtful, for she went on, 'Okay, we can't force her to have this, because we're not allowed to do anything to her without her permission, or your permission if she can't speak for herself, but do you want to take the responsibility on your shoulders if there's anything wrong with this baby at the end of all this, just for the sake of avoiding an episiotomy?'

Stephanie had obviously taken all this in, and of course, put like this, she didn't have much choice. She managed to say, 'Fine. Just go ahead and do it.'

Poor thing, I could see at a glance she was absolutely terrified of what they were going to do, and my heart went out to her. The look on her poor, pale, petrified face brought a lump to my throat, I took her in my arms and gave her a big hug, and promised, 'Don't worry, Stephanie, I won't let them do a big cut.'

Turning to the midwife I said, 'Okay, look, this is just the minimum cut, as small as possible?'

'Yes, she's not going to need a big cut.'

'And she's not going to feel this, right?'

'No, no, we give her an anaesthetic, same as she'd have at the dentist's, it numbs the area.'

'Okay.'

So they gave her an injection. I didn't actually look closely, but it seemed to me the needle was entering part of her vagina – it certainly wasn't in her bottom – and, though they did it at the height of a contraction, so she'd be thinking of that and not the injection, she must have felt it, she *must* have done. Still, even though she'd always hated needles of any kind, and panicked at the very thought of having a routine blood test, she didn't scream or holler out; and within about five minutes the midwife did the snip.

There was quite a lot of blood, but at the next contraction the midwife said to Stephanie, 'Okay, chin to chest, give us a good push.'

And at that most of the baby's head popped out, then with the very next push, the whole head crowned. It was absolutely amazing, there it was covered in quite dark hair, and now the little head turned so you could see the tiny face, the baby tried to gurgle as it turned, but seemed to choke, and afterwards Stephanie told me she felt its little legs kicking inside as it struggled to be free.

I bent down and touched the head, I cried, 'Oh Stephanie, it's here, the head's here, I've touched it!' and gave her yet another hug.

The midwife asked her, 'Do you want to touch the baby's head? . . . No? Oh, I see, you'd rather wait until it's cleaned up, right?' All this in response to Stephanie's frantic headshakes and nods.

And then the next minute the whole baby came wriggling out, a little girl, perfect, darling, gorgeous, there. They picked her up and flopped her face down by Stephanie's bottom, and clamped the cord, then put her up on Stephanie's shoulder.

What I felt at that moment is indescribable; such joy, a piercing happiness, I must have suffocated Stephanie as I put my arms round her and clasped her fast to me with the baby, the two of them pressed close. Then I burst into tears, Stephanie burst into tears, and I said, 'Stephanie, I love you, thank you, thank you, I love you so much, it's all over, it's all over, oh *thank* you . . .'

We carried on like this for about five minutes, howling and greeting, kissing and hugging; God knows what the midwives thought we were up to, but they didn't seem to suspect anything – I suppose they were used to all sorts of weird and wonderful reactions, seeing babies born every day. They'd said Mark could come in to witness the birth, but there was still no sign of him, so I dived out of the room to see if he'd arrived and somehow hadn't been able to find us. But when I dashed into the waiting room, the only person sitting there was Richard – the poor chap, he'd done nothing but wait, wait, wait so patiently all day long. I leapt up to him and flung my arms round him.

He lifted me up as I cried, 'It's all over, it's all over, I can't believe it's all over, she's fine, the baby's fine, she's gorgeous, a little girl . . . Mark's not here? I'll just go back in, see they're okay . . .'

I ran back to the delivery room. Everyone there was very busy, cleaning up, rushing round; they'd cut the cord and taken the baby away to the basin, wrapped in a blanket, to wash her head; then they put her in the small cot. I watched it all open-mouthed, totally absorbed, fascinated and exhilarated: I felt so privileged to have witnessed *anybody's* birth, let alone the birth of our baby. All the waiting, the months and months, weeks and weeks, days and days, was over, and so quickly. I was overcome, taken by storm, in shock at the speed and the thrill of it. The midwife had told me the time of the birth – 16.48. In under two hours, Stephanie had managed to push that baby out.

Now they were sitting her up and taking the gas mask off – yes, only now did she relinquish it, now she was sure the baby was born, though unbeknown to her, the midwives had turned the gas and air off fifteen minutes before the birth, to help her push better. As she sat up, she seemed to be coming to a little, and looked more lively.

I said, 'Are you sore, how do you feel?'

She only asked, 'Is the baby okay?'

'She's fine, Stephanie, how are *you*? Do you want to have a look at her?'

Turning to the midwife, I said, 'Can I pick the baby up?'

She said yes, go ahead, and I lifted the tiny person and held her up for Stephanie to see, and we both just sat there all goggle-eyed, staring at this wonderful little girl, with the tears streaming down our faces. As I held her in my arms she had her eyes wide open, she was all there, so lively and alert, she looked up at me and all round the room, taking it all in.

I couldn't believe it, but here she was.

But still no sign of her father. It was such a shame, I was so upset he'd missed the birth, these precious moments were trickling away without him – though considering I'd only called him less than two hours before, it was hardly surprising he hadn't arrived. That little baby had been born so fast, she'd caught us all off our guard, we'd barely had time to register that Stephanie was in labour before she was wriggling her way out and into the world.

Now the midwives were attending to Stephanie. The placenta hadn't yet emerged, and they asked if they could give her a Syntometrine injection to make it come away more quickly. Poor girl, she detested jabs, but by this time she was agreeing to everything; she was so *good*, so stoical, I'd have given anything to have gone through it for her, saved her all this further discomfort, but she didn't make a murmur of complaint, I was so proud of her.

Having made sure she was all right, I nipped out again to check that no one else had arrived. As I came out, Richard said, 'Is she all right? Can I see her?'

'She's great, but they're not letting anyone in there, they've said Mark can go in when he gets here, but no one else.'

'Well, there's still no sign of him . . .'

I ran to the window and drew back the curtains to see for myself, and lo and behold, just as I did so, there was Megan's car drawing up right outside. It had hardly stopped than Mark was flying out the door, and Megan leaping out the other side, the car doors left wide open as they ran to the entrance.

I raced to meet them and in my excitement got in a tussle with the main automatic door, for a moment neither I nor they could get through, I was waving madly at Mark through the glass and shrieking, 'It's all over, it's all over, the baby's here, a little girl, she's born!'

Next minute he was through the door and had me in his arms, he picked me up and whirled me round, we clung to each other and all we knew was happiness, happiness, happiness.

When we got to the delivery room, I put my head round the door just to check it was all right for us to come in. The head sister was there by this time, and more or less rounded on me and bit my head off the moment I opened my mouth.

'This is a very crucial time, we're trying to get the placenta out, so one of you either stay in, or get out. No, you *can't* both come in.'

I slipped out again and had a hurried and whispered confabulation with Mark about who should go in. Finally I said, 'Go *on*, go and hold your daughter,' and he did.

I stayed in the corridor with Megan and Richard, the three of us all hugging and crying together like total wrecks, and I told them all over again how wonderful it had been, how fantastic Stephanie was, how beautiful the baby was . . . The works. When I'd exhausted myself and them with that story, I started padding up and down the hall, wondering what on earth was going on in the room, for I'd glanced at my watch by now and realized Mark had been in there for about an hour and there was still no sign of them taking Stephanie and the baby out to the postnatal ward.

In a little while Mark came out and said to me, 'I think you'd better go back in. They're going to have to give Stephanie a spinal block, because the placenta hasn't come away and they're going to remove it manually . . .'

'Oh no, I don't believe it!'

As soon as he'd said the placenta wasn't separating from the womb, my heart seemed to stop dead for a second. This was part of the reason why I'd had a hysterectomy – because of complications associated with the placenta. I felt sick. I thought, 'No, no, please God, don't let this happen to her, nothing must happen to her!'

Mark could tell from my voice and the look on my face how I felt, and what I was thinking; and normally, he'd have hugged me tightly to reassure me and give me courage. But now we were up here, surrounded by hospital staff who thought he was Stephanie's boyfriend, we had to be very careful not to give the game away by a touch, a word, or even a look. It was terrible, trying to keep our distance from each other at such an emotional time, when all we wanted to do was express the overwhelming joy and love that coursed through every vein in our bodies.

Quailing inside, but trying to appear calm and cheerful, I joined Stephanie in the delivery room. By now she'd completely recovered from the effects of the gas and air, and had somehow managed to apply her make-up! She seemed very relaxed, and looked as fresh as a daisy; the prospect of the spinal block – an anaesthetic which would numb her in the back and uterus for a few hours – hardly seemed to bother her.

I exclaimed as light-heartedly as I could, 'I don't believe this, Stephanie! You've come through this whole thing with only gas and air and Pethidine, and now that the baby's born you've got to have a spinal block!'

'I know, I know – what a drag, eh?'

I managed to ask one of the midwives surreptitiously if there was a serious complication with the placenta – though I saw from the way they were letting Stephanie laugh and joke away that things couldn't be too dreadful. The midwife told me that it was nothing much to worry about, this sometimes happened; the placenta just didn't peel away of its own accord, so they had to take it out manually, since they'd already tried to stimulate its expulsion by giving her the Syntometrine injection and then – as Stephanie herself had just told me quietly – by putting the baby briefly to her breast to trigger the necessary hormone. Stephanie had warned me about this so that I wouldn't get a shock if someone else told me; we'd agreed in advance it would be best to avoid her breastfeeding the baby herself, to prevent bonding, but of course in this particular instance she'd had to let them try this in case it did help to expel the placenta. Again, I was amazed at how thoughtful she was; even at a moment like this, when most people would have been concerned with themselves, she'd been thinking of me and sparing my feelings. I was so grateful to her for everything, I prayed inwardly that this final stage of the birth process would go well without hurting her any more.

When I understood what they were actually going to do, I half-expected them to whisk me away, but to my surprise they seemed quite happy for me to stay, so I sat slightly to one side of Stephanie, holding the baby on my lap, letting her see everything – for like me, the wee thing seemed fascinated.

Stephanie was given the spinal block and her legs put up in stirrups. Not to put too fine a point on it, from where I sat I had a bird's eye view, and watched in astonishment as the doctor literally put his hand inside and took the placenta out in pieces. Stephanie didn't bat an eyelid, and joked with the doctor all the way through – but if she could have seen what I saw, she'd have been screaming her head off! However, it was soon over, and the doctor said she was now nice and clean inside, he'd made sure it was all out. I thought I'd start to faint when they stitched her up, but far from it – I was riveted to the scene, the whole operation was absolutely engrossing.

Then, while the baby and I looked on, the midwives gave Stephanie a bed-bath, and popped her into a clean nightie. By this time it was about six-thirty – delivering the placenta had almost taken longer than the birth itself – and getting on for the allotted visiting hour on the postnatal ward, where new mothers were allowed visitors between seven and eight in the evening. In normal circumstances, Stephanie would have gone straight through to postnatal and been able to see everybody then; but now, the midwife said she wasn't to go until the spinal had worn off, and couldn't see anybody else, apart from myself and Mark, until next morning.

I slipped out again then, to let the others know what was happening, and to give Mark another chance to go in and hold the baby, as I'd just had a long session with her – though I felt it would never be long enough, I'd never appease my hunger for holding her. I had to break the news to Richard that he wouldn't be able to see Stephanie until tomorrow. He was desolate, as all this time he'd been leaping up and down with anxiety and excitement, dying to get in there and see for himself she was all right. I really felt for him at that moment. I told him if we waited here for a while, he might just catch a glimpse of her as they wheeled her down to postnatal.

Sure enough, some time later, out she came, looking like a queen or some great lady, resplendent in her bed with a retinue of nurses and the baby in her arms like the most precious of gifts. Mark followed on a couple of paces behind, posing without too much difficulty as the proud father. As soon as this procession emerged from the delivery room, Richard, Megan and I ran after it like the traditional cheering crowd, all jostling for a better view. The staff, no doubt keen to get Stephanie and the baby settled for the night, pushed that bed pretty swiftly, so much so that poor Richard, who was certainly having a luckless night, was battered up against the swing doors as they thundered past.

And that was the first, and last, he saw of Stephanie until the following day. We hung around the hospital until Mark reappeared a while later, still wreathed in an evergreen grin he could do nothing to suppress.

'You finally let her go then, did you?' I teased.

'Finally.'

'Nobody else was getting a look-in while you were around, that's for sure.'

'Yes, I did tend to hog her a little.'

'A little. A little.'

'Well, I had to be seen to be the doting father . . .'

'Yes, that's true, that's true.'

'. . . Didn't want to be of course, just had to play the part.'

'Oh aye. How is she then?'

'Poor little mite, she was crying terribly to begin with, all she wanted was food, so I stuck my finger in her mouth while Stephanie was pumping the milk out, and the baby sucked away at it for a while and then bawled into a flood of tears because she suddenly realized she wasn't getting anything out. She was terribly upset to be tricked like this . . .'

'Oh, poor darling. Did her face go all bright red?'

'Yes, screwed up and bright red, just like yours when you have a tantrum!'

He added that she was fine now though, she was being fed; Stephanie was also comfortable and settled for the night. So, reluctantly, dragging our heels as none of us wanted to leave them, we headed off to a nearby hotel to wet the baby's head with champagne, and make all the phone calls to spread the good news. I spoke to Stephanie's mum and told her how marvellous Stephanie was, what a fantastic daughter she had, and how lucky I felt. She was very pleased to hear it had all gone well and Stephanie was fine, and said she'd see her when she came home in about ten days' time. This was a shame, but because of the fear of arousing suspicion, we'd felt we couldn't have too many visitors at the hospital or the cottage; and Stephanie particularly wanted us to be alone together for the final days before the parting, much as she'd have loved to see her mother at this time.

I rang off, and went back and joined the party. It was some night: from the hotel windows we could see fireworks going off all over the dark sky above the city, for it was 5 November, and it seemed to us that everyone was celebrating baby Kathleen's birth with showers of sparks and brilliant wheels of fire. It was the crowning touch to the most wonderful day of our lives, and by the end of our party, I don't think there was a dry eye in the house. Eventually we made our way back to the cottage, where Mark and I were at long last able to throw ourselves into each other's arms, completely enthralled with one another and the fact we actually had our daughter . . .

I guess we crawled into bed at about three in the morning. I was absolutely shattered, both emotionally and physically, but though my body was dying to pass out, my mind just wouldn't let go, I relived every single detail of those extraordinary hours over and over again. Each time my memory replayed the story, it was as if I'd never seen it before, the ecstasy and marvel of those moments were newborn. I lay awake all night, hugging my nuggets of wonder close to my heart, and even as I watched the morning hemming the curtains with new light it was no use, I could not sleep for joy.

11
PARTING

We were up early that first morning – I was going to say, 'bright and early', but in fact I felt shattered. I was hungover, I hadn't slept a wink, and inside I was both utterly drained from the emotional crescendo of the previous day and yet already starting to bubble up again with adrenalin. I was tense with the kind of longing and apprehension you feel at the start of a magical love affair – in my case, the relationship that had begun yesterday afternoon when I saw our darling daughter for the first time.

Richard, who was well on the way to being canonized by this stage for his saintly behaviour under almost unbearable emotional pressure, had agreed that Mark and I should go in first to see Stephanie and the baby.

We thought it would be best if the two of us weren't seen going about together too much in the hospital, so when we reached the town centre, Mark dropped me off and went on in for his visit, while I grabbed some much-needed breakfast and struggled to collect myself together. I found that on top of my excitement and aching need to see Kathleen again, I was also suddenly beside myself with worry about Stephanie's feelings for the baby. What would have happened overnight, during those hours she had spent with the little girl in the crib by her bed? I still felt so much for Stephanie – the deep, direct, uncomplicated love that had welled out of me for her as she'd laboured to bring the baby into the world was as strong as ever; but alongside it at that moment was this concern, my restless mind insisted on trying to flesh out with troubling visions the blank spaces of the night I'd been gone.

I tried my best to push these thoughts away along with my now-empty plate and coffee cup, and set off into town to buy Stephanie some flowers and a small gift. As I walked, in spite of my worries, joy buffeted me in great gusts, a fresh storm of happiness that made my eyes smart until the tears poured down my face. Wherever I went, joy went too, so that I wept as I chose three dozen pink roses in the florist's, and a box of chocolates in the newsagent's, and by the time I reached the hospital all my goods and sundries were almost awash with tears. I mustered some kind of composure until I got into Stephanie's room and saw her there with the baby. That started me off again in another squall of crying.

I kissed them both, and told Stephanie how well she looked, which was true; she looked fantastic, quite tired but so radiant, with a kind of in-built serenity that should have put all my niggling little fears to rest immediately. But still, it was an odd moment; for the first two minutes there I suddenly felt like a stranger, coming in and finding Mark well settled already, and Stephanie looking the picture of motherhood with the baby in her arms.

Mark was further over the moon than ever, if that was possible, and boasted, 'I've been taught how to change her nappy, shown how to bath her and whatnot . . .' Then, seeing my face, the shadowy doubt and slight traces of jealousy that must have played across it amid the joyful light, he quickly added, '. . . But I'm quitting as of next week, retiring . . . I'll start doing it badly . . .'

Instantly I retorted, 'No you WON'T!'

And, in that easy, instinctive way of hers, Stephanie made everything all right in a trice, by proffering me the baby and saying briskly, 'Now come on Rona, here she is, shut that door so no one can see, get the bottle and give her her feed . . . Mind her head now, there you go . . .'

It was the only moment when I felt nervous holding my daughter, and the nerves faded the minute I had her in my arms. As I fed her, Mark, Stephanie and I talked over the whole birth again, reliving it, taking out each precious moment and holding it up to the light, admiring and marvelling at the memories. It seemed a good time to ask the question I had to ask.

'Oh, Stephanie, how *are* you? How do you feel now you've actually given birth . . . You know, about Kathleen . . .'

'Rona, I feel *fine*. Of course I love her, but I haven't suddenly fallen *in love* with her, if you know what I mean . . . I look on myself as a babysitter, as if I were her auntie, she's lovely and I'm happy to look after her while I can, but I know she's your child. Obviously I'm very proud of her, I always will be, you see to me she's a work of art. I've created her and she's beautiful, but when I see the two of you with her, I know it's the fact you love each other so much that's brought her here, she is a *love* child, a miracle, the one good thing in my life that I've done.'

She spoke so naturally, the words were all unforced, I *knew* then there wasn't going to be a problem. My amazement at her strength and generosity of spirit deepened again, and was to go on deepening all through those last few days we had together. Every time I went in to hospital to visit, she'd immediately and easily pass the care of the baby straight to me, knowing without a word needing to be spoken that this was what I wanted. She seemed to read my mind now, we were completely in tune. On the night of that second day, I thought it best if I didn't spend the evening in the hospital, as I'd been there for hours that afternoon, and Richard, Mark, Megan and my mother were all visiting; I was still terrified the staff were going to rumble us. So I stayed on my own, having a solitary drink, and soon felt very left out and sorry for myself. When they returned, Mark brought me a special message from Stephanie.

'She sends you her love, and says she's thinking of you, she knows how hard this must be for you, but you're not to worry, everything is fine.'

I immediately felt much better and quite awe-struck by the girl. Here she was a day past giving birth, tired and very sore, and she made time to think of *my* feelings, reassure me . . . She was a superwoman.

Still, I never got used to the awfulness of having to leave her and little Kathleen behind in hospital at night; it was always a heart-wrenching moment, having to kiss Stephanie goodnight, then give Kathleen a last hug and a kiss. Luckily, we had arranged for Stephanie to have a single room, and the hospital was easy-going about daytime visiting, so Mark

had unlimited time with them, and I had pretty liberal access
– though, as I say, I was always on guard and wary of
spending the whole day there, for fear of someone putting
two and two together. So I compromised and just spent
eighty percent of my time there instead! It wasn't an easy
situation, all the same. Mark probably had the best of it, since
he was accepted for who he was – Kathleen's father; so even
though he had to keep whizzing back to work every other
day, whenever he *was* at the hospital, he could act completely
naturally (in other words, besottedly) towards his daughter.

But for myself and Richard it was a different story. Richard
was supposed to be Stephanie's brother, which rather put the
brakes on any unduly lovey-dovey cuddles between them;
and I was just passing as her friend and birth partner, so
I couldn't be seen to be totally obsessed with Kathleen, or
tongues might have started wagging.

And of course it was hardest of all for Stephanie. She was
apart from all of us at night – surely the worst time to be
left – and assumed by everyone to be an everyday, 'normal'
new mother, when in fact she must have been trying already
to prepare herself for the inevitable parting to come.

The situation wasn't helped by the staff's apparently uni-
versal bugbear about breastfeeding. Yes, they no doubt had
Kathleen's welfare uppermost in their minds, but it wasn't
as if Stephanie was categorically refusing to give her the
breastmilk. When she first registered at the hospital, she'd
told them clearly what her intention was; she wanted to
use the electric pump to express her milk for the baby.
She claimed that she had a repugnance to putting the baby
actually to her breast, but that by using the pump she could
still make sure the child received all the vital nourishment
and important antibodies from her milk – and expressing
it would enable her 'boyfriend' [Mark] to feed the baby as
well, giving her a chance to rest.

At the time, the nurses accepted this, but as soon as
Kathleen had actually been born, they changed their tune.
From the way they carried on, it seemed as if Stephanie
had no rights in the matter, and, as they became more and

more aggressive about it, that indeed she was some kind of monster who was depriving her child in a terrible way. It was almost as if they'd waited until she was at her most vulnerable, having just given birth, before launching their attack – and I don't think that's too strong a word for the 'persuasion' tactics to which they resorted.

On one particular occasion I turned up to visit Stephanie as usual, only to be asked to wait outside in the corridor, where I stood for an hour while one after another no fewer than six different nurses took it in turns to go into her room to lecture her about breastfeeding. One woman actually brandished a bottle of formula, which Stephanie was using to top up Kathleen's breastmilk feeds, and said, 'Look at this. This is cow's milk, it's intended for baby cows. Kathleen *isn't* a cow, she's a human being, and you've got the milk that's intended for her in your breasts, and you won't give it to her. You're being very selfish and very unfair to your child.'

I was beside myself with fury, but of course I didn't want to wade in and say my piece for fear of antagonizing them still further – especially as I was only supposed to be her friend, and nothing to do with the baby. Eventually Stephanie became pretty angry herself when one nurse had the cheek to suggest she see a social worker about it. Stephanie had them shut the door and then had what she later described as 'a bit of a chat' with some of the nurses – after which they kept out of her way and left her alone. But the whole episode was just another example of how much needless upset and unpleasantness are caused by the fact that surrogacy has been driven underground. Had we been able to tell the staff exactly what the situation was, not only would Stephanie have been left to pump away in peace from day one, but I could have started to breastfeed Kathleen myself during my visits, and she'd have had both the nourishment *and* the comfort of suckling.

For while all this was going on, I'd noticed that my own breasts now felt much fuller and harder, as if they were well and truly lactating. This had first happened on the day Kathleen was born, but at that point I could only guess at what was going on inside my body, because obviously

I didn't have time that day to use the pump. But the next evening I managed to have my usual 'expression session', and lo and behold, produced more than enough milk for one of the baby's feeds! Since I hadn't been able to keep up my regular pumping routine for a couple of days, I felt sure that this sudden gush of milk to my breasts was brought on by my overwhelming feelings for Kathleen – just as some breastfeeding new mothers experience a spontaneous release or 'let-down' of milk even when they only *think* about their babies. For me, this was just the icing on the cake – or rather, the cream on the top of the milk – to have our daughter safe and sound, and know that I was now capable of feeding her from my own body.

There was another lovely surprise in store. On the evening of the fourth day – that is, three days after the birth – I dropped Richard off at the hospital as usual for his visit and nipped into town to do a bit of late-night shopping before going back to collect him and say goodnight to Stephanie and Kathleen. But when I got to her room, expecting to find both her and the baby tucked up for the night, there was Stephanie up and about, fully dressed in the beautiful new tracksuit my sister had given her as a postnatal present, bag packed and ready to go! I couldn't believe my eyes. I said, 'What's going on, Stephanie, where are you going?'

She said, 'Come on Rona, get your daughter dressed, we're leaving tonight. I've asked the staff and they've said there's no reason for us to stay another day unless we want to, I've had my final check-up and been discharged . . . I wanted to surprise you.'

She'd certainly succeeded! I was thrilled, but at the time I panicked. I cried, 'Oh no, I haven't got everything ready at the cottage, I haven't got the sterilizer out, I haven't double-scrubbed everything . . .'

'Well you'd better hurry up and do it all quick, because Kathleen's coming home right now!'

With shaking hands I managed to slip Kathleen into her minute clothes, the miniscule bootees I'd bought for her, then wrapped her in a warm blanket, and we were off. As we got in the car, the midwife who was seeing us out of the hospital handed Kathleen to Stephanie, who held her all the way back to the cottage, as I was driving.

But the minute we reached the house and had opened the door, Stephanie turned to me on the threshold and gave me the baby, saying simply and tenderly, 'There you go, Rona, there's your daughter.'

I broke down, Stephanie did too, and we stood in the doorway with me clasping this tiny child and hugging Stephanie and crying for joy all at the same time. That moment was so precious, I don't ever want to forget it, or lose the memory of the overpowering love that swept through me then. I felt truly blessed to have shared with her in the whole amazing experience, and as we looked down together into Kathleen's delicate face, wave after wave of sheer wonder and delight surged up, broke and ran through my every vein in quicksilver pulses of happiness.

Later that night, when we'd all calmed down a little, had some coffee, admired Kathleen some more, and reminded Stephanie of how wonderful she was, I rang Mark, who was back at home working until the following night. I said, 'Mark, Kathleen's home!'

'What do you mean she's home?! She's not meant to be out till tomorrow at the earliest!'

'No, no, she's here now, they've come home, Stephanie wanted to surprise me.'

'I wish I could be there, you lucky thing you . . .'

'Yes, Kathleen's going to be sleeping in the bed with me tonight, I can't believe it but she is, and you're not going to be here, it's such a shame!'

'Well, I'll be there at the speed of light tomorrow, don't you worry. I'm the one who's supposed to hog her, remember.'

That first night with Kathleen I didn't sleep a wink – and not because she kept me awake. No, it was the marvellous novelty of her that made it impossible for me to settle, I was like a child on Christmas Eve, unable to keep from peeking at this little treasure. I kept kissing her and touching her lovely skin, and inside I was whispering over and over to myself, 'You're *here*, you're *here* . . .!'

I tried to turn over and doze off, knowing I should get some rest, but it was hopeless: there was no way I was going to sleep with this beautiful little baby lying next to me in the bed.

The next night Mark arrived, laden with vintage Moët & Chandon, so we had a wee party to celebrate Kathleen's homecoming, drinking the sublime champagne out of mugs, as there were no glasses in the cottage. At last we could all be together again without having to worry about keeping up appearances – which was just as well, as what with lack of sleep and an overdose of excitement, we were all pretty zombified by this time.

I think we must have survived those days on sheer exhilaration and a tremendous sense of sharing together in this most momentous event. Richard and Stephanie were fantastic, they really kept the whole show going so that Mark and I could spend as much time as possible with Kathleen. Richard magicked up endless meals out of thin air, and was quite happy to take the baby now and again to give her a feed if Mark and I were sleeping or out shopping.

'I'm practising for when Stephanie and I have our own fifteen,' he'd say.

Quick as a flash, she'd be on to him, 'Fifteen. I'll see you later.'

For her part, Stephanie was as sensitive, tactful and helpful as anybody could ever have been: I just couldn't get over it. I think we'd probably all wondered, secretly, how these days would go, especially in relation to caring for the baby, but any fears we might have had just vanished when we were actually living together in that situation. Stephanie was always careful to ask before she picked Kathleen up or did anything for her, but there was no jealousy or tension between any of us about it, it all seemed to come so naturally – I suppose because Stephanie was making it so clear that Mark and I had nothing to worry about. I was so glad that she seemed to be happy – not just resigned or grinning and bearing it, but genuinely happy. At any moment I half-expected her to suffer the notorious 'baby blues' and come down with a great thump, but it simply didn't happen. Maybe she was lucky, and her hormones didn't do whatever dips and dives cause such depression; but personally, I think she made her own luck, her sheer strength of character saw her through.

Because she loved the baby, there was no doubt about it; on the day after we came back to the cottage, she'd given me a card congratulating Mark and me on our new daughter, and inside, along with the good wishes, she'd written, 'Please tell her I love her.' This was something she was very anxious we should explain to Kathleen when she was older; that Stephanie did love her, she hadn't given her up because she didn't care, but for the opposite reason – because she knew that we would adore and cherish Kathleen all our lives. I know this preoccupied Stephanie, because she told me she'd been worried that I might not accept the baby as my own – something that never crossed my mind. It was a fear I think she lost the moment she saw my face when Kathleen was born, and any remaining traces of doubt must have disappeared for good during the days we spent together after the birth. She said she'd also wondered whether she'd be able to cope with watching me bond with the baby, but when it came to it, the more I showed my love for Kathleen, the happier Stephanie felt.

I think she quickly saw, too, that my whole family had accepted Kathleen immediately as part of the clan: Megan had arrived on the day of the birth, and my mother had rushed down to the hospital to see Kathleen and Stephanie the day after, and the expressions on their faces spoke volumes more than mere words ever could. I hope that Stephanie also realized how they felt about *her*, how proud we all were of her and of what she'd done for us, and that maybe this helped boost her ego a bit.

At any rate, I remember those six days we spent together after she'd left hospital as a very happy, relaxed time; though we were all tired, there was also a sense of achievement. We had accomplished at last what we'd set out to do, and this brought peace to us all. I guess it was an inner peace, because outwardly, we were pretty busy; Mark was still flitting to and from work (he was saving the rest of his leave for our return home), I was caring for Kathleen, Richard was manning the cottage, and Stephanie was expressing milk for the baby like nobody's business now she'd finally got shot of the nurses' Gestapo. We both wanted Kathleen to have the best possible start in life, and though I was putting her to my breast now, my milk supply still wasn't sufficient to provide all her needs. So every three or four hours, Stephanie would plug in to the pump and express enough for several feeds, which she'd then bottle and store in the fridge. This meant that at night, whenever Kathleen was hungry, all Mark and I had to do was nip to the kitchen and get out a bottle. Then, first thing in the morning, Stephanie would knock quietly on our door and whisper, 'Has she finished all those? Yes? I'll just go and do some more then.'

Kathleen seemed to have a pretty voracious appetite, so Stephanie was kept hard at it, but though it must have been tiring and quite sore using the pump, she never complained or flagged. Around the third day, I came down with a vicious bout of tonsillitis and had to take to my bed. Stephanie was just marvellous, keeping my spirits up, taking care of Kathleen whenever I felt too exhausted, yet never assuming anything or swooping down and carrying her off simply because I was ill. She was so sensible, calm and cheerful; over and over again I wondered at her, and again I reproached myself for all my earlier, harsher feelings towards her during parts of the pregnancy. I felt I knew her so much better now: in the past couple of months, I'd come to understand her far better than in all the long year before. I knew now that when the time came I'd be able to tell Kathleen so much more about her birth mother than I'd ever thought possible, and hopefully convey to her what a special person Stephanie was. I hoped too that in these last few days Stephanie was starting to know how I felt about her, and glean something – comfort, happiness, I didn't know what – from that awareness.

Meanwhile, another recurrent routine in our lives was the daily round of 'musical beds', otherwise known as the mid-wife's visit. Each morning, Stephanie would get up first thing and have a bath, while Richard either shut himself away in their room or slipped out until the midwife had gone. Just before she arrived – usually around ten o'clock – I would leap out of bed and make myself look vaguely human, and Stephanie would go into our bedroom, where Kathleen was sleeping and where most of the baby things were, and take over for the duration. By and large, though slightly strenuous, this set-up seemed to work like a charm; Stephanie was sure they'd rumble her every time they asked her about her 'boyfriend', because she said it always took her a few seconds to remember what she'd told them last time; but if anyone did suspect, they certainly didn't let on. The only hair-raising moment was on the second visit, which was the first day Mark was back at the cottage. At one point the midwife started talking to Stephanie about the name she should write down for the baby on her form, and Stephanie was telling her to use Mark's surname even though they weren't yet married. Just as she said this, Mark suddenly remembered he was still wearing his wedding ring – in fact, to his dismayed stare, it seemed to be sitting there positively glowing out the message 'I'm married, I'm married'! However, he covered it with his hand, and the midwife seemed not to have noticed, so we all lived to fight another day.

It turned out that the health visitor wouldn't be calling until at least the eleventh day – that is, the day after Stephanie had been finally signed off by the midwife – by which time, of course, we would all have gone our own ways, as we were due to part on the tenth day. So Stephanie asked the midwife what she should do in the event of her having to move; she said there was a strong possibility that in a few days' time, her 'boyfriend' would be posted to work elsewhere and she'd be going with the baby to join him. The midwife said that as long as they were moving after the tenth day, there'd be no problem; Stephanie should register the baby with a doctor as soon as possible after the move, and the health visitor would see her after that. All Stephanie's medical records concerning the birth and so on would be transferred from the hospital to her doctor, so the health visitor would know all about both her and Kathleen's condition to date.

So that was that little hurdle overcome. The next item on the agenda was to get Kathleen's birth officially registered, which we did on the ninth day. I was still laid low with tonsillitis, but we only had ten days in which to register the birth, and we also had to get the registration done before Stephanie left us for good, so Mark and Stephanie took Kathleen into Dundee and had her registered there. Stephanie explained to the registrar that she wanted the baby to take her father's name as they 'intended to get married', so she was registered in our surname, and her parents as Stephanie Cottam and Mark Walker. Stephanie was given the full, long birth certificate with all the details of parentage, as well as the basic one just citing Kathleen's name and date and place of birth. Both these she passed to me on her return from Dundee. I must admit I felt a twinge of sadness when I saw the names on the certificate in black-and-white, and knew that mine could never be included; it was hard to accept that my part in Kathleen's conception and birth had no official recognition, would be unacknowledged forever. I felt momentarily excluded, and moped about a bit for an hour or so by myself until I got it into my head that, after all, it was only a piece of paper and a few words. And what were those by comparison with the whole lifetime of shared experience and love that lay ahead for me with Kathleen?

Still, that ninth day was a gloomy one in other ways. Since I'd been ill I'd been sorely conscious of how, lying in my bed, I was wasting the precious last days we all had together, days that would never come again. Though we hadn't done anything particularly dynamic or spectacular during this time, the hours had just flown past, spent in a simple, implicit communion of mutual happiness and peace which had a special purity I treasured, knowing it was unique, particular to that overwhelming moment in all our lives. Ironically, this period that in anticipation, before the birth, I'd thought would weigh so heavy on my hands, now in reality seemed so short – was, indeed, almost gone. Now the moment of parting was almost upon us, I didn't want it to come, I didn't want to say goodbye.

We all felt it; as the days passed, an unspoken sadness came creeping in, and by that ninth day it was there, hovering over us, very close, inescapable. At one point I spoke privately to Richard about Stephanie, not wanting, now, in these last hours, to confront her with the pain, but needing to speak of it, to ask him how he thought they would go on from there, and how we should actually map out the parting to suit her best. She'd gone through so much for us already, I was anxious to find a way of saving her any more suffering.

Richard said he wasn't sure how they would tackle the next few weeks – whether it was best to go right away for a holiday, or to let Stephanie rest and mull over things for a while. All he knew was that she felt very strongly that she didn't want to be cast aside by us now that it was all over – she was worried that she'd never hear from us again and it would be as if none of this had ever happened.

I could see why she was concerned, because at the very start we'd said we thought we'd have to make a clean break. But now I couldn't even contemplate that, it would be terrible, and I said, 'No, no, that's not going to happen, we couldn't do that. Anyway I feel I could cope much easier if I knew Stephanie was okay and we did stay in touch, at least for a wee while until you're both settled and I'm sure she's getting on all right. As long as she's happy to see us, I think we should all meet up at your wedding, and then maybe at the COTS Annual General Meeting in April. After that we'll take it from there . . .'

He seemed very relieved. He said that as far as the following day was concerned, the only thing he knew for definite was that Stephanie didn't want to be the last to leave the cottage; she wanted to leave *us*, rather than us leaving her. We agreed it would be best if my sister, who was coming down to see them off anyway, drove them to the airport where they'd catch a flight back to their home town.

In the evening, somehow, without a word being spoken, the four of us all sat down together. Soon, we began to voice our shared thoughts about the morrow – how sad it was, and how quickly the time had gone; almost without noticing it, we'd spent the past year of our lives together, and tomorrow was goodbye. A pall of misery seemed to hang over the room, and though we tried to lighten things with a few half-hearted jokes, we all felt trapped. In our hearts, I don't think any of us wanted to say farewell to such good friends; yet we also knew that this had to be. Kathleen couldn't have two mothers, and we all had to forge our independent futures. This was an experience that we would never forget, but difficult as it was to part, we couldn't hang on to each other now and try to keep it alive, it just wouldn't be natural.

Still, as we were all getting ready for bed, I went to Stephanie with Kathleen in my arms and asked her if she would like to take her for that last night. I had no qualms at all about doing this: it was an offer I made with all my heart. I wanted her to know how absolutely I trusted her, but more than that, I knew she had been hiding her feelings so as not to hurt me by showing her love for the child, and I wanted her to have the chance to say her goodbyes properly, privately. I didn't want her to have to live with the regret of never having said to Kathleen what she felt for her – she was going to have a hard enough time without that. It was only when Stephanie looked at me as I proffered her the baby that I suddenly thought how my gesture, intended in kindness, might seem cruel; for her face showed her great sense of loss. But I hope she understood that I had never meant to wound her, for she answered calmly, 'Rona, I would love to have her for the night. But I think I'd better not.'

That night, I wrote her a long letter, a letter from the heart.

Dear Stephanie,
I've thought and thought of a special way to say thank you but there's just no words to express how I feel inside right now. The depth of happiness I felt on Kathleen's birth will remain with me for ever – only *you* saw my face at that magic moment of birth so only *you* will know what she means to me and Mark.

I'm sorry, Stephanie, that we didn't all get along so well at the beginning – I'm sorry Mark and I did not make more of an effort to be like a family for you and see that you were crying out for more companionship. I hope you will understand it was difficult for me in the beginning – I didn't want to put myself in a position where I could easily get hurt again – losing another baby would have ended me. I thought if I didn't get too close I wouldn't get so hurt – it's such a shame I didn't know you then – the you you are now – that side of you was hidden or sadly, perhaps I just didn't see it.

What I want more than anything else now is to be assured of your happiness – I need to *know* you are happy and can go forward from here with no regrets. You are such a unique person Stephanie, the dedication you have shown towards helping me and showing me Kathleen was really ours has been 100%. Never once did you give us any reason to fear losing her and that took *guts* – I know it – we both know it. Don't *ever* drag yourself down again Stephanie please. You went into this with heart and soul, I know your family will be proud of you when they really know what happened.

Tomorrow I think will be the hardest day of our lives – to say goodbye to you will be unbearable – I will try to be strong but I know I won't succeed. One thing you must always remember, Stephanie, is Kathleen *will* know how much you love her – do not despair any more about this – she *will* be told as she grows up and will be given all the information she wants. She will always know, please, please be assured of that.

I look at Kathleen each night with tears in my eyes – I still can't believe we have a daughter and such a beautiful one – miracles *do* happen – now I am totally complete, contented and happy. I will keep in touch as much as I feel I can – it's a strange feeling now of not wanting to let go, but thinking it is best to do so – I'm very mixed up about this as I discussed with Richard. I want to do the right thing for all of us. Sometimes reviving the past brings back too many painful memories. Right now I don't know. I do know that you will always be in our hearts and our thoughts. If I could give you the world right now I would, but how can one repay the priceless gift you have given us?

Please promise me that you will hold your head very high Stephanie – go out for all that you want in life – you deserve the best and I know you will find it. Please also promise me that you will come to us if you ever need any kind of help – you know we all care for you very, very much and will be wanting to hear how you are doing in the new flat. We'll talk to you I hope on Xmas Day so until then Stephanie, please please take care and be happy. The joy you have brought to Mark and me means more to us than anything in the world.

We are both privileged to have known such a special person.

All the love in the world,

Rona

The night passed, and the last morning broke. The midwife came and went, and discharged Stephanie and Kathleen. There were small things to be done. We wrote Stephanie's card, collected a bouquet of flowers, and wrapped her presents; Mark and I were giving her a little gold locket with two photos inside – one of herself and Richard together, and the other of Mark and me, both taken at my sister's wedding the previous July. Then we went round the cottage, checking that we'd got everything packed and cleaned up. Nobody moaned or wailed or even wept openly yet, but we were all crying inside, aching with the knowledge that the inevitable moment had come.

So we sat down and drank each other's health, and toasted the slumbering Kathleen, and marvelled again at her innocent face. We joked and fooled around a little, trying to fend off the sadness. The worst thing was we had no special reason to leave at that particular time; the cottage was booked for another three days, and Richard's and Stephanie's flight wasn't for some hours yet, so there was no spur to force us to get up and go. Eventually, during a lull in the conversation, we all looked at each other as if to say, 'Is this it? Will I stand up now?'

I went into our bedroom and brought out the flowers and presents, and gave Stephanie the bouquet and the letter, which I told her to read later, when she was home. Megan gave Richard Stephanie's present from all of us, and told him to keep it safe for Stephanie to open at home, it was something special we wanted her to have, another locket, a beautiful one that had been in the family for some time. Then Stephanie opened our present to her, and asked me to put it on for her; I unfastened the chain and put it round her neck, and our tears began to fall. Hugs and kisses were exchanged all round the room; I handed Kathleen to Stephanie for her to say goodbye, she hugged the little girl tightly and with a final kiss handed her back to me. Somehow we got to the door, but I couldn't let go of Stephanie now, I'd latched on to her hand, and in the street passed Kathleen to Mark so I could hug Stephanie properly.

I took her in my arms and kissed her over and over, thanking her, thanking her through my tears, and I don't know if I'd ever have let her go had someone not murmured, 'Come on, time to go now, time to go . . .' in a soft, embarrassed whisper. The car doors were open, the engine running, I hugged Richard and begged him through my sobs to look after Stephanie, take care of her. Then he got in, Stephanie got in, I took Kathleen again and ran to the front seat and bent to kiss Stephanie one more time and hold Kathleen for her last farewell. Then, quickly, finally, inevitably, the doors were shut, the car pulled away, I saw through a blur of tears sad hands waving whitely from the windows, Mark put his arms round me and I turned my face into his shoulder and cried out with the unbearable pain of it, cried as though my heart would never heal.

For what seemed a long, blind while we stood trembling together in that torn time. Then Kathleen stirred between us in the wintry air, and all folded in each other's arms the three of us made our way for the last time up the cold path and into the empty cottage.

12
COMING HOME

During the drive home I had a long time to think about what had happened. It was odd: for so many months I had longed for this day, wished the hours away to this moment, and now the moment had come and I was on a real downer. I knew that no matter what happened in the future, I should never forget Stephanie and what she had done for us. I knew also that I would always remember her with love, that somewhere deep down we were now inextricably bound together, so that parting from her had left a grieving mark that would never quite fade. Yet though I'd initially feared such a hurt, now it had happened I could not regret it. For it was a loss borne of the love and joy we had shared; a glad, sad scar close to my heart.

And despite my sorrow, as we drew nearer to home, I was filled with eager excitement. Incredibly, our dream had come true, and here we were pulling up outside the dear, familiar flat I hadn't seen for weeks, and stepping over the threshold with our daughter in our arms. It was strange and lovely to be home again, alone again – yet not alone, because now we had our very own child. Already, though she slept on peacefully through our arrival, the quiet breath of her presence cast its spell; everything was the same, yet unutterably altered. I recognized it all, and felt the warmth of that recognition, yet still it was as if I saw everything for the first time. It was a strange and wonderful moment: as if life were truly starting anew.

Now too Mark and I could rediscover our relationship. At last we could touch and kiss each other again whenever we wanted, without having to wonder who might be watching, or asking ourselves, 'Can I do this – who am I meant to be at the moment?' The past fortnight's subterfuge – the terrible time of pretending half the day to be just friends – was over. We were home, together, ourselves again, with no lies to tell and no prying eyes to see us.

It was late by the time we'd unpacked, and we were so tired, we soon got ready for bed. The simple acts of going into the nursery and taking out the little nightclothes we'd bought for Kathleen made my heart dance with delight, and it danced even more when I noticed that Mark had put up the lovely friezes we'd chosen together – putting the finishing touches to the room while I'd been at the cottage, to surprise me on my return! Then we climbed into bed, Kathleen in the moses basket beside us. All night I kept waking and peeping over to see she was still there, for I simply could not, could not believe it.

And she's still here, thank heaven, as I write this, almost four months later – here in spite of all our fears that she would somehow be snatched from us once we informed the health visitor. I know that other couples in our situation may have had bad experiences with the local authorities; but for us, so far, the reverse has been true, and our earlier terrors now seem, if not groundless, then at least exaggerated.

We took Kathleen to register her with our GP more or less immediately after returning home. I'd already spoken to him about the fact we were having a surrogate baby when I'd consulted him about breastfeeding, and he assured us now that he'd pave the way for the health visitor, and everything we'd told him would be strictly confidential. I'm sure he kept his word, but in fact the health visitor to whom we were assigned turned out to be none other than the one who'd seen me when I was pregnant with the twins, so of course she knew what had happened to me and quickly twigged what was going on. However, she was very sympathetic, as was the woman who took over from her while she had to go into hospital for a time. They both assured us that what they knew would be kept absolutely within the four walls of their office, and that as far as anyone else was concerned, Kathleen was an adopted baby. They've gone out of their way to put our minds at rest; one of them even rang the social services on our behalf, to ask if she was under any legal obligation to inform them that she knew of a surrogacy case in Aberdeen. The social services replied that as long as she is satisfied with the care the baby's receiving, they do not need, or wish, to intervene. The health visitors have also agreed if necessary to supply affidavits attesting to our worthiness as Kathleen's parents, should we need these for the custody or adoption hearing; and all in all, we couldn't have asked for more support from them.

Encouraged by the social services' response to our health visitor's enquiry, I subsequently telephoned them myself, anonymously, and outlined the situation. They told me that there is no need for us to worry; they understand our predicament, and will do nothing until we apply for adoption, when they will simply follow the necessary procedure. Far from seeking to obstruct us, they wished us all the best for the future! Another phantom fear has been allayed.

We're presently in the throes of deciding when to apply for adoption. The legal aspect of surrogacy has proved to be even more of a minefield than we thought – the one thing that has turned out worse than we anticipated. Shortly after we brought Kathleen home, our solicitor sent a paternity writ to Stephanie, stating that Mark was Kathleen's father and would be applying for custody of her. Stephanie had twenty-one days in which to contest this, and, as previously agreed, she duly returned the writ uncontested, together with a letter from her solicitor confirming this, stating that she gave Kathleen up willingly, and furthermore, thought it in the child's best interests that Mark should be granted custody.

In the meantime, as advised by our solicitor, we had Mark's paternity confirmed by genetic (DNA) fingerprint testing. The writ, and the result of the test, will be sent to the sheriff court with our application for a declarator of paternity – in other words, legal recognition that Mark has been found and declared to be Kathleen's father – and for a formal award of custody. (This is a Scottish legal procedure.) The writ makes no mention of the fact that Kathleen was born through surrogacy – though our affidavits imply this.

If the court grants Mark custody, he will then have the same rights over Kathleen as any other father of a child born to married parents. As far as we know, we're the first couple in the UK to make use of this law in a surrogacy case. It prevents Kathleen from being removed from our care unless by order of a higher court, and means that we will at least have safeguarded our position legally as far as possible until we have adopted her.

As far as the adoption is concerned, we await legal advice as to the best time to apply. We will be applying to adopt Kathleen using the procedure called 'adoption by a relative', which will involve trekking through another jungle of administrative paperwork and red tape. Our solicitor will write to inform the local authority of our intention to adopt Kathleen. Then the authority's home-finding team will visit us at least once a week for a period of thirteen weeks, and report back to the solicitor. These reports will then be sent to the adoption panel of the court, possibly together with affidavits from us, Stephanie, the health visitor, and someone else who knows us well, testifying to our good character and fitness to be parents. Meanwhile, during the thirteen-week period, both we and Stephanie will also be visited by a curator *ad litem*, who will ascertain that we are all happy to go ahead with the application; and his or her report will also go back to the court. Stephanie will have to sign a form consenting to the adoption, and will then have a further six weeks in which to change her mind.

And finally, when all these documents have been submitted, the adoption hearing will take place in private. The adoption could be approved there and then; or, as our solicitor thinks likely, if we apply too soon, the court may impose an interim period of one year on it, in order to ensure we will have been married for at least two years by the time we adopt, and to investigate our situation in more detail in view of the fact that it's a surrogacy case. The decision rests entirely with the individual sheriff who will hear our case – some may be sympathetic to surrogacy, and some may not.

There are further legal complications. Because of the ambiguity and inadequacy of the existing Surrogacy Act, lawyers are now uncertain as to how best to proceed in order to minimize the chances of surrogate children being made wards-of-court by the social services. While we know of no case in Scotland where this has happened, and I have actually been reassured by the social services themselves, we've been advised by an eminent solicitor who has dealt with several surrogacy cases in England that social services there have been issued with a blanket directive to make surrogate babies wards-of-court. If this were to happen, we should then have to fight our case in the High Court – and face exorbitant costs.

At the moment, our solicitor and this eminent lawyer are consulting together; but although it's unlikely our application to adopt won't be granted eventually – after all, Mark *is* Kathleen's genetic father – and no one could remove her from our care unless we were proven to be ill-treating her, the fact remains that until we have applied for and been granted adoption, we don't have full parental rights over her in law. We'd have to fight our case in court should Stephanie meanwhile inexplicably change her mind.

Mercifully, amid all the uncertainty and anxiety created by the tangled web of the law, Stephanie changing her mind isn't something we have to worry about: we're surer of her than ever. My feelings for her have remained unchanged from the day she handed me our daughter; I hold her in deep respect and love. In January Mark and I were guests at her wedding to Richard; sadly, Kathleen had been under the weather for a few days beforehand, so we had to leave her in my sister's besotted care for the day, but it was lovely to see Stephanie looking so well, and both she and Richard truly happy. They told us they'd had some difficulties with certain members of both their families about Stephanie having been a surrogate, but they were weathering the storm, and I hope and believe Stephanie will sail through, especially with Richard by her side. She has a heart of gold, but she's tough with it. I know – because I saw it and she told me herself – that this experience has changed her: in her words, not mine, she feels 'a better person' for having done this, and to me

she seems much calmer, and, I think, more truly confident.
I trust she thinks more highly of herself now – because she
is unique, a very special person, and I feel privileged to have
known her.

As to the future relationship between us, we know nothing
for sure except that we intend meeting at the COTS AGM in
April. After that, we'll have to see. As I told Stephanie in my
letter at the parting, I have mixed feelings – one half of me
says it's best to drift apart, the other half doesn't want to
lose her. This is the one cruel blow about surrogacy: a baby
can't have two mothers, and for Kathleen's sake above all
else we need to lead separate lives. We'll keep in touch, send
Christmas cards and so on, because I know she wants that;
and of course, when Kathleen's older, she'll know the truth
– we'll keep our promise to Stephanie on that score, and
Kathleen has every right to know about her genetic mother.
But at the same time, we must keep some distance. Stephanie
and Richard intend having their own family; and Mark and I
must bring up ours independently. Rightly or wrongly, I feel
my position as Kathleen's mother would never be completely
secure if we all remained very close while she was growing
up. I don't mean to imply anything about how Stephanie
would behave, for I've no worries there. But I don't want
to be reminded always that I couldn't give birth myself, and,
without lying, I want to be accepted as Kathleen's mother,
something I can't do properly if she's constantly seeing her
birth mother. So, although part of me regrets it, I don't see
us having a lifelong relationship with Stephanie and Richard.
Mark may well be posted abroad in future, and I guess then
the friendship might gradually peter out. But no matter what
happens outwardly, inside, we won't forget.

For thanks to Stephanie, a wonderful sense of content-
ment has permeated our lives. The three of us – Mark,
Kathleen and I – are now well and truly settled in our
family life, and Mark and I are just amazed at how easily
we've slipped into parenthood. Everybody warns you that
a new baby will bring a huge upheaval in your life, and I'd
had visions of myself tearing my hair out, knee-deep in dirty

dishes with a crying baby, but this simply hasn't happened. Of course it *is* a tremendous change, and a full-time job, looking after a baby, but it doesn't seem to be hard work. Partly this is because Kathleen is such an easy baby – she only cries if she wants to be fed, or a bit of attention, or she's got a wet nappy – she doesn't whinge. And after all, motherhood is something I've waited an awful long time for. I've wanted so much for us to be complete as a family, that now we are, I feel totally fulfilled, relaxed and happy – and I think perhaps Kathleen senses this and feels secure.

Mark and I are also very lucky in that we had such a lot of experiences in the first year of our marriage, it's really cemented our feelings for each other. Mark loves to be doing things for Kathleen as much as I do, and since his working hours are quite varied, he's often at home for part of the morning or the afternoon, which means I can have a lie-in or dive into a hot bath while he's with Kathleen, and I don't have sole responsibility for her all day long like many mothers. I also have a lot of support from both our families, all of whom absolutely dote on Kathleen. They're always popping in and somehow, as if accidentally, finding they can stay just that bit longer and give her her feed, or another cuddle . . .

So we both love parenthood. Perhaps we appreciate Kathleen more because we had to fight so hard to have her. She's such a joy, if anyone came to the door tomorrow and offered me another baby to look after as well, I'd welcome it with open arms and say, 'Yes please! Another two!' I think, probably, I was just meant to have children.

The pleasures are so simple, yet so profound. I love going out for walks with her in the pram, pushing it up and down, and I'm so looking forward to the summertime and trundling round the park – all the idyllic things that a baby represents are coming true for me, and if I died tomorrow I'd go happier than I've ever been in my whole life.

Kathleen has brought such a sense of purpose to me. I feel I can go forward now, and I wasn't before – and without her, I don't think I would have done. My thoughts of Emma are with me still, and they're very very deep, but I simply haven't as much time to dwell on them, and the restless, terrible sadness that used to drive me out of my bed to pad up and down the floor weeping all night has calmed – I've not done that since Kathleen was born. Though I'll never forget Emma, I know now that as the years go on, the acute pain of losing her will eventually subside.

Kathleen has solved so many problems, she's so good for us. And yet she's definitely *not* a replacement, I hope nobody could ever think that. She's herself, her own individual person, and so cheerful and contented, I'm sure she's going to grow up to be a really relaxed, happy-go-lucky little girl, and it gladdens my heart, because I was quite withdrawn and shy as a child. Kathleen just isn't like that: she gurgles away all day long. When we visit the baby clinic they always say, 'I've never seen this baby cry, are you sure she knows how to?'

I love just to look at her, I feel I'll never tire of watching her lovely, rounded face with its small snub nose, dark blue eyes, and Cupid's bow mouth with the little indentation above the upper lip, just like Mark's (only not hidden by a moustache . . .) She has a beautiful, smooth skin, and in her sleep her whole face has a lovely, peaceful glow, like the softest candlelight.

She brings so many special moments, like the day I'd been pulling faces at her and suddenly her eyes opened wide and her whole mouth smiled, not in her usual windy smirk but a real, first, heart-stopping smile. Or like the evening I was in the kitchen, Kathleen was sitting with Mark in our bedroom, and I could hear that – in between teaching her her two times table and singing 'Old Macdonald had a Farm' – he kept saying to her, 'Hello, hello . . .' All of a sudden he gave a great shriek, and I ran to the bedroom thinking something awful had happened, and there was Mark crying, 'Rona, Rona, she said it, she said "hel . . . lo", "hel . . . lo", a double-barrelled one, she said it to me twice!'

Quite simply, it's hard to isolate single moments as special, because every minute shines now. But perhaps my favourite of all is first thing in the morning, when I hear her move and wake to see her looking at me with that big beaming smile, and my heart just melts with the most wonderful feeling in the whole world.

Kathleen, and Emma, are my first reasons for writing this book, to remember all the precious moments they have brought to our lives; and so when the time comes Kathleen will know her own story from its very beginning – there'll be this testament for us all to turn to.

I have also written this book in the hope that it will take us one more step along the way to drawing the whole subject of surrogacy out of the darkness to which it is presently consigned by the Government's reluctance to deal with it properly in law. Though few people realize it, surrogacy has been around for hundreds of years – probably for as long as there have been childless couples, and women who were prepared to bear them children. And it is not going to go away. However much the Government may stall and evade the issue, by declaring, in documents such as the 1987 White Paper on Human Fertilization and Embryology, that there 'will be no provision for licensing non-commercial surrogacy services and . . . any contract drawn up as part of a surrogacy arrangement will be unenforceable' – nonetheless, surrogacy is here to stay. Ignoring it, or simply hoping to make it as difficult as possible, will only drive it deeper underground, and lead to more damage and disaster for people who have already suffered the despairs of infertility. For surrogacy, which gives life, is as unstoppable as life itself; you may as well try to stop the ceaseless tide from beating at the shore as quench a childless couple's urge to have a child.

If the Government has now recognized that in certain cases, nothing will prevent a woman who doesn't want a baby from terminating a pregnancy, even if she has to risk her own life to do so, then surely the Government must see also that the desire to *create* life burns just as strongly in the hearts of many people, and it must legislate for surrogacy to continue in properly controlled conditions. Certainly, surrogacy presents a complex human problem, fraught with tangled emotions, and surrogate children face a potentially more difficult family history than those conceived under 'normal' conditions. But is their history more problematic than that of adopted children or children conceived by artificial insemination by donor? Is it any harder to come to terms with the fact that you have a genetic mother and a nurturing mother, both of whom love you, who eagerly and deliberately sought your conception, than it is to accept that your genetic parents could not, or would not, keep you, or that you will never know who your genetic father is? The plain fact is that in various ways, our society already tacitly acknowledges that blood is not always thicker than water, and that a happy family can grow from more than just one's own flesh and blood. However, if we persist in believing – as I do myself – that the natural genetic family is the ideal, why then make such options as host surrogacy almost impossible, legally, and so prevent more couples like us from having their own genetic children? IVF techniques can only be described as a modern-day miracle, a scientific advance to be applauded and marvelled at. To date, there have been thousands of IVF ('test-tube') babies born, but only infertile women who still have their wombs have been offered such miraculous opportunities. Those who, like me, have ovaries, but no physical means of carrying the developing baby inside their bodies, face the inexpressible frustration and heartbreak of knowing that the only thing preventing them from having their own genetic children is an ambiguity in the law concerning host surrogacy. Yet, compared with straightforward surrogacy, hosting is not only preferable for the couple; it must surely make the surrogate's life easier too, for she then gives back to the couple what was theirs in the first place, rather than bearing and parting with her own child.

People argue that surrogacy is potentially exploitative and dangerous – mainly for women, but also for the couple, should the surrogate seek to blackmail them, as well as for the child, who could be used as a pawn or sold for money.

Of course this is true – *as long as it goes unsupervised* and without proper legal provision. But a legalized, non-profit-making surrogacy scheme, handled, as adoption is, by local authorities, could minimize the risk of exploitation and greatly reduce the medical hazards for everyone concerned, especially the mother and child. Such a service could screen both the couples and surrogates, physically and psychologically, and provide expert counselling to ensure that everyone entering into a surrogacy arrangement was both fit and ready to do so, and understood exactly what was involved. An impartial, disinterested, mediating body could prevent each party in such agreements from exploiting the other. It could ensure that all children conceived in such a way would be properly cared for, before conception, during pregnancy and birth, and afterwards, and their best interests secured. Just as adopted children can now trace their genetic parents, so a similar provision could enshrine this right for the surrogate child. If such a service existed, instead of finding themselves at odds with society's expectations, these children would be more readily integrated, because people would accept openly that surrogacy was an option for infertile couples.

With the help of such a scheme, instead of being perceived as evil, ignorant, loose, feckless, cold, calculating, or money-grabbing, surrogate mothers might also be understood for the unselfish, extraordinary people that many of them are, and the true dignity and strength of which some women are capable would be acknowledged. For, as we learnt through our experience, there *are* women like Stephanie who are prepared to conceive and bear children for couples essentially for the sole purpose of making them happy, and not for financial gain. A state-funded surrogacy scheme could ensure that the surrogate was properly provided for during her pregnancy – for it's hardly acceptable to expect women to enter into surrogacy, which will prevent them from working for at least a few months, without some guarantee of support; and in any case, the better fed, housed and nurtured the mother, the better the chances of the baby being born safe and sound. This kind of provision would stem the tide of commercial surrogacy, to which, personally, I am opposed;

I feel that as long as people, especially third parties, are exchanging large sums of money in such deals, as happens in the United States, the child's interests in particular cannot be guaranteed.

Finally, such a service would recognize a woman's right to use her own body as she saw fit, while simultaneously helping to ensure neither she nor the child suffered from the consequences of her decision to be a surrogate. Surely, under such a scheme, far from being exploitative, or encouraging women to sell themselves and their children to the highest bidder, surrogacy would acknowledge not only women's unique power to bear life, but the special capacity of some to share that gift with others less fortunate than themselves.

If there were such a service – and, for all the potential complexities of setting it up, I still believe it is feasible, especially if it were treated as an extension of existing infertility services – I feel sure that, slowly maybe but surely, people's attitudes towards surrogacy could change, *would* change. Unfortunately, it looks as though we're in a vicious circle at the moment – such a scheme is unlikely to develop until the Government's attitudes change, and the best way to change those is . . . by having such a scheme. But we have to make a start somewhere.

This book is a cry against the darkness of ignorance and fear in which surrogacy is presently shrouded: a cry from both my head – I've tried to give some rational arguments – and my heart. I hope that anyone who is sceptical of surrogacy and has made it through this far into my story now at least has some food for thought. To such people I say: I can't pretend I wouldn't like to convince you that surrogacy is a good thing, and should be legalized – I would. But since I may not be able to do that, I accept you've a right to your views; feelings about all matters of life and death run very high, and spring from the gut. But I would make a plea. Please don't knock surrogacy, don't knock other people who want to do it – give them the right to make their own choice. It's a difficult choice, and they'll have gone through one hell of a lot of heartache to make it; so please don't bring them down any more.

And please be a bit more sympathetic towards people who've taken this big step. Everybody solves their problems in different ways, and luckily most people can solve their infertility through medical science. But for the few of us who can't, and want to take this road, please don't stand in our way; allow us freedom of choice. We're not out to take advantage of any poor young girl who doesn't know what she's doing; and we're not destroying life, we're creating it where otherwise it couldn't be. We don't go into this lightly, so please don't tell us we could adopt, when there are no babies for adoption, the lists have been closed for years, and won't reopen until it's too late. Above all, don't tell us fate has dealt us this blow and we should learn to live with it. Fate isn't something which is totally in the control of the gods – I don't believe in that sort of destiny. It's my understanding that if you simply go along with what's happened to you, then it's fated your life will not improve, you will be stuck with what has happened. There are events in life too cruel to be accepted, and they strike at random and without warning. In such circumstances the only use for notions of destiny is to believe your fate – if you must use such a word – is to find a way out of the situation. Had I not thought that, to this day I should still be pacing the floor at midnight, grieving for the ghost of my dead child. Instead of which, I'm writing this, while our baby laughs at me from her bouncer, reminding me to entreat all doubters to do one last thing – just thank your lucky stars you *can* have children.

EPILOGUE

Last, but not least, I have written this book for all the hundreds of couples who have faced, or are facing, similar dilemmas to ours, and are maybe contemplating surrogacy. This isn't a DIY manual on the subject; it's a personal account, but if it helps just one couple in any way, it will have been worth it. For anybody who's reading this, and is perhaps excited at the thought of it, it has to be said – don't look at surrogacy through rose-coloured glasses. Your experience may be different from mine. But take heart in the knowledge that if you put your heads and hearts together, and you really want to do it, you can. You must have support, and be strong; and you must do whatever is needed for your surrogate, however hard it seems. Always remember what she's doing for you, and what she's going through in order to do it. Together, if you make an effort, the three of you can find the best in each other, things you didn't even realize were there. Surrogacy will spring its surprises on you – not least, as we found, the strange fact that you *can* turn off feelings of resentment, and in so doing, discover a spontaneous liking for someone you would never otherwise have really known.

Surrogacy is a major experience, full of wonderful, wonderful moments, and also of awful, tragic ones – and you'll have your share of those along the way. But always remember, when things have gone wrong and you're in the depths of despair, that at the end of the day – and it's not *that* far off – you're going to have your daughter, or your son. And all the months of waiting, and all the months of tears, will fade away into insignificance when you see that little life and hold your baby in your arms.

STOP PRESS

At last! On Wednesday, 14 March 1990, the British Medical Association (BMA) gave doctors the go-ahead to assist in surrogacy cases. They also gave IVF ('test-tube' baby) clinics the green light to use a surrogate to carry the child of an infertile couple.

I never thought this day would come – COTS has been campaigning relentlessly for years to achieve this. My spirits have soared – there is hope yet!

How happy I am for all the couples considering surrogacy, and for the surrogates themselves. They will now at least have some dignity, and the essential opportunity to confide in their doctor, discuss all the potential pitfalls and voice their ceaseless anxieties about their experience of surrogacy. At long last all of us who have been involved in surrogacy arrangements can begin to come out into the open, to stand up and fight for what we believe in and want – and not be afraid to do so.

Of course this is only one small step along the path towards true acceptance. The law must now be clarified, to take account of the BMA's decisions and guidelines, and the eventual adoption of the child eased so that parents of surrogate babies no longer live in dread of the implications their surrogacy arrangements may have for their application to adopt.

Is it too early to say the nightmare is over, and my brightest dreams may yet come true?

※   ※   ※   ※   ※

Following the birth of Kathleen, Peterkins (Solicitors), for and on behalf of Mr and Mrs D. Cameron, raised a Sheriff Court action for Declarator of paternity and custody. Decree was granted on 1 May 1990. Mr and Mrs Cameron have now instructed their lawyers to petition for the adoption of Kathleen.